MOMS
WHO STAY AND FIGHT

MOMS

WHO STAY AND FIGHT

How to Raise
the Next Generation of
HEROES

KRISTYN TRIMBLE

CFI

AN IMPRINT OF CEDAR FORT, INC.
SPRINGVILLE, UTAH

ISBN 13: 978-1-4621-2181-6

Published by CFI, an imprint of Cedar Fort, Inc.
2373 W. 700 S., Springville, UT 84663
Distributed by Cedar Fort, Inc., www.cedarfort.com

LIBRARY OF CONGRESS CATALOGING-IN-PUBLICATION DATA

Names: Trimble, Kristyn, 1982- author.
Title: Moms who stay and fight : how to raise the next generation of heroes /
  Kristyn Trimble.
Description: Springville, UT : CFI, An imprint of Cedar Fort, Inc., [2017] |
  Includes bibliographical references and index.
Identifiers: LCCN 2017055388 (print) | LCCN 2017058606 (ebook) | ISBN
  9781462128754 (epub, pdf, mobi) | ISBN 9781462121816 | ISBN
  9781462121816 (perfect bound : alk. paper)
Subjects: LCSH: Child rearing--Religious aspects--Church of Jesus Christ of
  Latter-day Saints. | Child rearing--Religious aspects--Mormon Church. |
  Motherhood--Religious aspects--Church of Jesus Christ of Latter-day
  Saints. | Motherhood--Religious aspects--Mormon Church. | Church of Jesus
  Christ of Latter-day Saints--Doctrines. | Mormon Church--Doctrines.
Classification: LCC BX8643.C56 (ebook) | LCC BX8643.C56 T75 2017 (print) |
  DDC 248.8/431--dc23
LC record available at https://lccn.loc.gov/201705538 8

Cover design by Jeff Harvey
Cover design © 2018 Cedar Fort, Inc.
Edited and typeset by Erica Myers, Sydnee Hyer, and Kaitlin Barwick

Printed in the United States of America

10 9 8 7 6 5 4 3 2 1

Printed on acid-free paper

I dedicate this book to the three people in my life
who enabled me to become a mom who stays and fights.
To my loving and supportive husband, Greg,
to my sweet and hardworking daughter, Taylor,
and to my son, Trenton, who always keeps me laughing.
I love you all more than you'll ever know!
I also dedicate this book to my mother, Vicky Burnham,
who was the greatest example for me of a mom who stays and fights!
Thank you for all that you sacrificed for me.
I love you for it!

CONTENTS

FOREWORD

by Al Carraway

Award-winning speaker and best-selling author of
More than the Tattooed Mormon and *Cheers to Eternity*

Growing up, I was never even around children or babies. I'm the youngest of three, and my cousins are not too far behind me in age. Not only were babies foreign to me but for the most part there were no examples around me that motherhood was something to work toward. I never knew anyone with a large family, and definitely no one I knew had ever heard of forever families, myself included at that time.

I was always the awkward one that really would tell you no if you offered to let me hold your baby, and after I told your toddler "Hi!" I'd be at a complete loss for words. I literally had no idea how to talk to them. Everything about kids made me uncomfortable. I 100% didn't want to be a mom at any point of my life growing up. Not that I was actively against it—it was just foreign to me. I just didn't get it. I didn't get why anyone would *want* to have kids.

Parenthood and homemaking just wasn't emphasized in our New Yorker culture. From the youngest age, I can remember *only* being asked what I was going to do with my life, what kind of career was I going to have, how was I going to support myself? A mentality in New York is, no one will do it for you but you, so you gotta figure it out. So I never thought about getting married and starting a family. No one else I knew did either. It was all career oriented. And of course there's a "but" coming.

But then I learned about and fell in love with God. And I learned very quickly that there is so much more to life than what I thought. And then I fell in love with a man I ended up marrying. And although I was adamant about waiting at least two years after being married to have a baby, it was just a month after we knelt at the altar that God told us otherwise.

After nine months and forty-three hours of labor, my first child was born. Right when she was born, I saw my husband's reaction before I ever saw our daughter. He broke down into tears and just collapsed on my stomach. And all of a sudden, *I got it.* In that exact moment, I finally understood the importance of families. She was the first baby I had ever held in my life. She looked me in the eyes and I felt the Spirit. I felt, more intensely than ever before in my life, physical love and approval from God.

And now, we're about to celebrate our second child's second birthday. I've heard and learned a lot over the years. And here's what I decided: Don't let people tell you marriage becomes boring. Don't let people tell you kids ruin or take away from things. Don't let people's comments of "once you get married, you can't do this" and "once you have kids, you won't be able to do that" discourage you. Because they simply are not true.

I absolutely love everything about having kids. Adventures have doubled since we've had ours, because we chose to plan it that way. Life is better experienced with others. Experiences are richer when shared. Humor is perfectly there for the good and the bad.

I'm sure most of us can admit to spending time thinking about the things we wish were different about us or our life, or maybe even our kids. I'm sure we can all admit to letting the adversary run rogue with our thoughts and what we wish we had or were better at, or what trial we wish would pass, or if only we could go back to *that one time,* or fast forward to another time. Perhaps you can admit to feeling like you must live up to some sort of expectation or standard with family and parenting. Perhaps you have lost count of how many times you weren't good enough because you were doing things differently

I am not a typical "Mormon mom," although I'm not really sure what that means anyways. I can count on one hand how many times I've cooked dinner; I'm terrible at it. I don't desire a ton of kids; I'd be happy with just the two I have now. I work full time and Ben stays home with them. That's what our circumstances allow right now at this stage as Ben is in school.

And that's okay.

But it's not about me, our family, or our situation. And it's not about if you work or stay home with your kids. And it is most definitely not about being a "typical" anything. Because it's not, and never will be, about comparing yourself to anyone. It's about your life being okay too. However it may be.

Let's celebrate you not being the "typical." Celebrate and embrace and be proud of your differences. Being different is an amazing gift! If we were all the same, how stupid would that be? We wouldn't get anything done. We wouldn't progress. Celebrate your womanhood with confidence knowing that the best thing we could ever be is ourselves and who God wants us to be. Celebrate knowing He is in charge and He does not make mistakes.

Embrace yourself, your life, and your role—whatever it may be. Embrace and love who you are and where you are. There is something amazing and needful and profound at every stage of your life. Keep being you. Keep laughing. Keep praying. Keep trying. Keep growing. Don't exhaust yourselves trying to live up to this "perfect" image *someone else* created for your life. Stop thinking perfect is a thing and don't drink the poison of comparison. Because it is oh so unhealthy to you *and your soul.* Exist to be happy, not impress. Because life is too short not to love the journey God has for you. Because life is too short not to see yourself the way He sees you. And who He sees you as is someone capable of becoming like Him.

There are a lot of things I don't have and that I'm not good at. But I like me. And God likes me. And my husband and kids like me. And we have a lot of fun together doing whatever we want to do. *And my soul is dancing within me and OH what a feeling!*

And I want to be the one to tell you, in case no one else has yet—

Life is *amazing*! Marriage is amazing. Parenting and kids are absolutely amazing. Happiness exists in the mundane *and* the hard. Beauty is in the unexpected. Trials are adventures. Happiness exists because God exists. And He lives to help you succeed.

In the final days of my pregnancy with my not-yet-born son, I had received a priesthood blessing that just so happened to mention him. I was told that he and my daughter, Gracie, picked me to be their mom. I was told that he had watched over me throughout my life. I was told that he missed Ben and I, and was very anxious to be reunited with us, especially Gracie. He and Gracie were inseparable before she was born. I was told Gracie would recognize him when she saw him. I was told that Heavenly Father knew I'd been thinking about how many kids I should have. I was told it was up to me and whatever I decide—but that Gracie and Christian were necessary.

Goosebumps.

Often when we think of families we think of the here and the hereafter. It's not often we stop and think that we were all united together already before here. And this has nothing to do with actually birthing a child or not, but about family overall, whether in reference to your parents and siblings, those that you adopt or foster, members of the church or not, alive or not yet or no longer, etc. It doesn't necessarily matter *how* our families are brought together here on earth, it matters that we existed and interacted and loved *beforehand*. And now as families we are watching over and helping. We are interacting, learning, growing, and loving. Each unique. Each necessary to God. For experiences and lessons intertwined between us that are too intricate to fully understand, to reconnect us from *before*, to help us grow *here*, and to prepare us for the *hereafter*.

Though perhaps reading this we can recall too many times to count when we have all felt that deep and eternal connection to those in our family and their influence on us, some during little everyday things, and some through sacred and personal experiences or blessings, whether they are acting on this side of the veil, or the other.

So what's my point?

My point is that we are not alone.

Not only is God absolutely always and at all times mindful of us, but He has also blessed us with family on both sides of the veil as well, watching over and cheering for us—unseen protection and guidance from those anxious to be born, and from those already passed.

My point is that was not the start of me and my soon-to-be son.

This life is not the start of you.

My point is we need to take care of each other. We are together for a reason. How we spend our time with those in our family and extended family, the ways we act and react with them, and the opportunities we take to teach and extend love is crucial. It matters and can and does ripple into the eternities.

I want to be the one to tell you, in case no one else has—

You and your efforts are important. They matter. They don't go unnoticed. Your life has purpose. It has deep meaning. It has Godly help and support available at *every* stage of your life. And you do not need to be any more of anything to feel of Him, to be loved by Him, and to receive the best ever created by Him.

I'm elated you picked up this book! I'm elated at the efforts to improve. Kristyn does an amazing job at this comprehensive look at the challenges, blessings, and responsibilities associated with the high and noble calling of being a mother. Parenting is absolutely worth the effort. It is guided by God. And He *will* help us with the steps to become better and to live the life He would have us live. A life full of purpose and growth and happiness!

PREFACE

by Greg Trimble

*"There are few things more powerful than the
faithful prayers of a righteous mother."*
—BOYD K. PACKER[1]

Rise and shine. Rise and shine." These were the words I'd hear every day for my entire childhood. They were the words of my mom. Just as she had welcomed me into this world, she would welcome me into each and every new day by asking me to "rise and shine."

I never comprehended the meaning behind those words. I don't know whether she carefully chose those words for their deeper meaning or whether she just wanted me to get my lazy behind out of bed for school.

Either way, as I ponder the meaning of those words today, I realize that there is nothing more that she would have wanted me to do in my life than to "rise and shine" in everything that I did.

To "rise" to the occasion and to "shine" for the whole world to see.

After rising from my bed in the morning and getting ready for the day, I'd get in the car and we'd drive to school. Before I got out, my mom would deliver, without fail, her second daily phrase:

"Have a good day, do good things, be a good boy!"

As you read these things, they probably don't mean a lot to you. But I can hear them ringing in my ears for all eternity.

My mom, having endured a tortuous and painful pregnancy with me, brought me into this world to do a few simple things: to "rise and shine," to have good days and be happy, to do good things for other people, and to be a good boy. In effect, my mom summarized God's entire plan for me while simultaneously teaching me the essence of "pure religion" as defined by James (James 1:27).

That's what moms do. They reflect the love of our creator and push us to reach our full potential. They ask us to rise up in the face of evil and make a stand. They ask us to let our light shine before men and not place it under a bushel. They ask us to have joy, to serve others, and to keep the commandments.

All of this they ask of us so that we will be happy. Their happiness depends on our happiness. Their empathy knows no bounds.

They give up their lives for the sake of another and then love them without question, without equivocation, and without conditions.

Mothers are "types" of Christ.

When I wrote my first book, *Dads Who Stay and Fight*, most people probably wouldn't guess that the person most responsible for the things I wrote in that book—about fatherhood—was a woman. My mom. Of course, I learned a lot from my dad, but it was my mom who was there, day in and day out. She woke me up in the morning and she tucked me into bed at night. It was from her that I received the majority of my training.

I didn't realize it at the time, but my mom was subtly and consistently teaching me to be the kind of man, the kind of dad, that she never had in her life.

To say it plainly, my mom didn't have a "dad who stayed and fought." At age 10, my mom was rendered effectually without a dad. The world had grabbed ahold of him, a family meeting was held, and just like that, he was gone.

Throughout my entire childhood, she never spoke of him. I never even thought to ask. It was as if he never existed. It was nothing to me, but to her . . . it must have been a lifetime of mental and emotional pain.

My grandma Arlene was left alone to raise a sixteen-year-old boy and two innocent daughters: my aunt, who was thirteen, and my mom, who was ten. My grandmother's pain, distrust, and embarrassment wore a happy mask for all those many years as well.

I can't imagine how my grandma must have felt knowing that she—and she alone—would have to be the nurturing mother and homemaker as well as the physical, spiritual, and emotional mentor and protector of her three children, who depended on her for everything. How alone she must have felt, and how scared. The mental anguish of these new realities had to have been even heavier to bear than any upcoming hardships they would experience in the years to come due to the lack of a father and companion in the home.

My grandma stared into the darkness and clawed her way out of the abyss to be a mom who stayed to fight!

I never remember a time during my childhood and adolescent years where "Grandma G" (Arlene) wasn't there. She lived with us for my entire life.

I will never forget, to my dying day, the old shrill holler from her bedroom every time she heard me rushing down the stairs to leave for school or baseball practice. She would cry out, "Gregory, make sure you be of good cheer!"

This, from a woman who had every reason, every excuse, not to be of good cheer, to wallow in the misery of her past rejections and heartbreaks! This from one of the earliest of women to serve a mission for the church—who had every right to expect a peaceful and happy life.

She reached into Doctrine and Covenants 68:6 to remind me to be of good cheer. At the time, I never wondered how many times she had to remind herself of that scripture just to keep the wheels turning in her life.

I didn't just have one strong mother in my life. I had two remarkable women who taught me how to become the man I am today. Above all, these women wanted me to be happy. The words of this favorite song of my mom has summarized what she's wished for me in life. Play it for her and she'll melt:

> I hope you never lose your sense of wonder
> You get your fill to eat but always keep that hunger
> May you never take one single breath for granted
> God forbid love ever leave you empty handed

I hope you still feel small when you stand beside the ocean
Whenever one door closes I hope one more opens
Promise me that you'll give faith a fighting chance
And when you get the choice to sit it out or dance
I hope you dance.[2]

That is the essence of a mom who stays and fights. She wants her kids to live and to dance. To laugh and to cry. To learn and to grow and to subsequently become a mom or a dad who stays to fight for their family.

That is what this world needs more of: more moms and dads who stay and fight the fight!

REFERENCES

1. Boyd K. Packer, "These Things I Know," *Ensign*, May 2013.
2. Lee Ann Womack, "I Hope You Dance," recorded September 1999, track 2 on *I Hope You Dance*, MCA Nashville. Compact disc.

MOMS WITH PURPOSE

"Motherhood is near to divinity. It is the highest,
holiest service to be assumed by mankind.
It places her who honors its holy calling
and service next to the angels."
—J. REUBEN CLARK[1]

I n my living room there hangs a beautiful painting. A painting that, in my mind, perfectly symbolizes women's divine purpose and calling as mothers. I bought this painting while I was still somewhat of a young and immature youth—a couple years before I was married, and definitely before I had children of my own. Its meaning to me at the time of its purchase has since grown, deepened, and evolved as the years have passed and my life has developed.

The painting is of a massive lighthouse, towering over the rocky ledge to which it holds fast. Unmovable, unshakable on that impenetrable foundation upon which it's standing. Cruel and unceasing waves beat down upon its curved alabaster walls—and yet it still stands, unmovable, unshakable. Evening is drawing nigh, and the storm clouds are gathering, but the brilliance emanating from this great edifice radiates light to all that are within the reach of its influence. It stands as a stone-faced light unto the darkening world that surrounds it—still unmovable, unshakable.

My twenty-year-old self looked at this painting with envy. I wanted more than anything to be that lighthouse. I desired with all my heart to be as rock solid upon the foundation on which I was built. I longed to hold fast—no matter how strong the waves were that beat upon me. I craved to have my spirit be as white and pure as the walls with which it was made. I hoped to be so full of light that I couldn't help but radiate that light to those who came within my sphere of influence.

I loved this painting. I knew I needed to own it.

The thing that's most interesting to me is that at the time I first purchased the painting, for some reason, I only took notice of half the picture. Sounds strange, but it's true! I suppose because of the time of life I was in—being a single young woman—the rest of the painting was meaningless to me, so I didn't give it a second glance.

Now, years later, gazing over this stunning picture, I couldn't imagine the oil-stained canvas without the second half. The meaning of the painting expands tenfold when the two parts of the painting are combined.

Attached to the far side of the lighthouse is a home. A simple little cottage that looks happy and content despite the roaring of the waves and the gathering storm clouds outside of its protective walls. A golden glow is emanating through the paned glass of the windows, which gives the painting a sense of warmth and cheerfulness. I can tell there is deep love within the home. I'm certain of it!

Now, when I gaze upon this painting, I no longer see just a single lonely lighthouse standing strong and firm against the harsh elements that fight to tear it down. No. I see the true vision behind this inspired painting. This vision has brought meaning and purpose to my life. It's what pushes me each and every day to be a better wife, a better mother, and a better daughter of God than I was the day before.

Within the borders of this painting I see a mother standing strong and firm upon the bedrock of her faith in Jesus Christ. I see her radiating the light of her faith and the love for her family to all that are within her sphere of influence. I see this mother reaching out her strong protective arms to shield her little home from the crashing waves of the world that desperately seek to destroy those she loves most. I see great strength of character, wisdom in her understanding, nobility within her nature, and deep abiding love within the heart of this good mother.

Within this picture, I see the woman I fall short of being every day. But also, within the borders of that canvas, I see the woman I am striving to become. The woman I know I will someday be.

Mothers, our purpose is vital to the Creator's plan. We are called to be the teachers, exemplars, nurturers, and spiritual protectors of all of God's children, but especially of those we have been given special charge over. If we don't give our all—our everything—to teach the next generation to rise above the trash of this world, who will? If we don't teach our children how to distinguish between gospel truth and the deceit of Satan, who will? I shudder at the thought of moms passing the responsibility of this great calling on to the wisdom of the world.

If all children had mothers who raised them with love—teaching them how to damper their physical appetites by letting their spiritual natures take the lead; teaching them kindness, strong work ethic, and exemplar moral courage—there would be little need for jails, homeless shelters, addiction recovery programs, weapons manufacturers, police departments, armies, and navies.

I see the great strength, power, and influence women have over every human being that enters this world. We have a short eighteen years to shape, mold, and influence these children through our teaching and examples, and then we have to let them go take on the outside world and pray that they have taken to heart the lessons of honesty, kindness, virtue, sacrifice, hard work, and courage that we have tried our hardest to instill in them.

The rising generation is our only hope to change this harsh world! They are our future leaders in government, leaders in business, leaders of religion. They are our future! If we want an honest world, we need to raise our children to be honest. If we want a kind world, we need to raise our children to be kind. If we want a virtuous world, we need to raise our children to be virtuous. Mothers have the power to change the world one child at a time.

Who will stand with me and give their all in order to fulfill their divine purpose?

REFERENCE

1. J. Reuben Clark, *The First Presidency Message*, October 1942, http://emp
   .byui.edu/marrottr/FirstPresOct1942.htm.

MOMS WHO AREN'T "GOOD ENOUGH"

"We must have the courage to be imperfect
while striving for perfection."
—PATRICIA HOLLAND[1]

I don't think it will come as a shocker to any woman when I state that I believe one of Satan's strongest strategies for the downfall of Heavenly Father's daughters is to make us believe that we can, should, and need to achieve perfection on our own. We feel the need to be perfect wives, perfect mothers, perfect homemakers, perfect in our church assignments, perfect in our community roles, and on top of it all, we need to look perfect while doing it all! Whew . . . I feel worn out just talking about it!

Satan whispers in our minds that the unachievable pursuit of self-perfection is achievable and we are weak, not worthy, and not good enough if we cannot make it happen ourselves. He does what he always does: he tells us lies mingled with scripture. We read the words, "Be ye therefore perfect" (Matthew 5:48), spoken by our Savior, and Satan twists those words in our minds to make us feel like it is up to us to do all the perfecting ourselves. We put every last ounce of effort into doing all that we think we are supposed to do and then, right when we are getting used to the load, more gets plopped on top of us . . . then more . . . then more still, until finally we feel like we are failing in all aspects of our lives. We are tired both mentally and physically and just want to yell out, "I quit!" to the world. It is at this point that we are at our weakest, and it's right where Satan wants us.

Sister Patricia Holland once made the following declaration: "If I were Satan and wanted to destroy a society, I think I would stage a full-blown blitz on womanhood. I would keep them so distraught and distracted that they would never find the calming strength and serenity. . . . Too many of us are struggling and suffering, too many are running faster than they have strength, expecting too much of themselves."[2]

This is personally one of my biggest "thorns in the flesh" (2 Corinthians 12:7), as the apostle Paul would call it. My husband, Greg, would agree wholeheartedly with me, and it seriously annoys him to no end! I see the good in everyone around me, except, of course, myself. I have a much easier time seeing all my flaws, faults, failures, and lack of talent than any good that's contained within me. I tend to focus solely on the negative things, like the one month I forgot to do my visiting teaching, rather than on the numerous months that I actually did it. Then I feel a gnawing sense of guilt for it. I focus on the time I got upset at my kids for this or that, instead of on all the time spent with them teaching them, holding them, and reading to them. The overwhelming feeling of guilt returns. Then I will look around my house and see dirty dishes in the sink, laundry that isn't finished, scriptures that haven't been picked up that day, a stringy mop on top of my head and . . . "Oh wait, what, it's dinner time already and all I have is frozen chicken in the freezer . . . I guess we're having cold cereal tonight, family. Whoops!" The weight of my inadequacies jump out at me like one of those creepy jack-in-the-boxes I was terrified of as a kid. The sad thing is that I think this is true for most, if not all of us moms. If you don't have days like this every once in a while, then congratulations! You are better than I am.

Stephen E. Robinson, in his inspiring book *Believing Christ*, described a time in his family's life when his wife, Janet, no longer could deal with the immense pressure for perfection she felt throughout all the aspects of her tremendously busy life. He explained, "One day the lights just went out. It was as though Janet had died to spiritual things; she had burned out. She became very passive in her attitude toward the Church."

He went on to say, "Janet wouldn't talk about it; she wouldn't tell me what was wrong. Finally, after almost two weeks, I made her mad with my nagging one night as we lay in bed, and she said, 'All right. Do you want to know what's wrong? I'll tell you what's wrong—I can't do it anymore. I can't lift it. My load is just too heavy. I can't do all the things I'm supposed to.' . . . She just started naming, one after the other, all the things she couldn't do or couldn't do perfectly—all the individual bricks that had been laid on her back in the name of perfection until they had crushed the light out of her."

Janet continued explaining to her worried husband, "I try not to yell at the kids, but I can't seem to help it; I get mad and I yell. So then I try not to get mad, but I eventually do. I try not to have hard feelings toward this person and that person, but I do. I'm just not very Christlike. No matter how hard I try to love everyone, I fail. I don't have the talent Sister X has, and I'm just not as sweet as Sister Y. Steve, I'm just not perfect—I'm never going to be perfect, and I just can't pretend anymore that I am. I've finally admitted to myself that I can't make it to the celestial kingdom, so why should I break my back trying?"

Stephen then asked his wife, "Do you have a testimony?"

She responded, "Of course I do—that's what's so terrible. I know the gospel is true, I just can't live up to it. . . . I try, but no matter how hard I try, I don't seem to be able to do all that's asked of me."[3]

He went on to explain that he knew his wife. He knew she was one of the sweetest, most loving, and selfless people he had ever met. But all his wife was able to see within herself was her faults, inadequacies, and her imperfections. She couldn't see the woman inside herself who was trying her hardest to be like the Savior—all she saw was the woman who failed at it.

President Uchtdorf, knowing just how hard we women are on ourselves, stated at the General Relief Society Meeting of General Conference:

> I want to tell you something that I hope you will take in the right way: God is fully aware that you and I are not perfect.
>
> Let me add: God is also fully aware that the people you think are perfect are not.

And yet we spend so much time and energy comparing ourselves to others—usually comparing our weaknesses to their strengths. This drives us to create expectations for ourselves that are impossible to meet. As a result, we never celebrate our good efforts because they seem to be less than what someone else does.

Everyone has strengths and weaknesses.

It's wonderful to have strengths.

And it is part of your mortal experience that you do have weaknesses.

God wants to help us to eventually turn all of our weaknesses into strengths, but He knows that this is a long-term goal. He wants us to become perfect, and if we stay on the path of discipleship, one day we will. It's OK that you're not quite there yet. Keep working on it, but stop punishing yourself.

Dear sisters, many of you are endlessly compassionate and patient with the weaknesses of others, please remember also to be compassionate and patient with yourself.[4]

I don't know about you, but when I read these words by President Uchtdorf, I breathe an instantaneous sigh of relief. To know that I don't need to be perfect right now—at this very moment—is very comforting. To know that all I need to do today is work towards being a *little* better. That I can do. That I feel is possible.

The most important thing we can do for ourselves is try to recognize which way we are facing on the road to perfection. I always picture life being likened to a person who is trekking upstream in a raging, thrashing river. Our destination is way up stream, far beyond the scope of our vision. The only way for us to get there is to push through the murky, enraged river with all our might. Taking one tiny step at a time, moving inch by inch toward our destination of becoming like our Heavenly Parents. The rapids come and regularly knock us down and push us off course, making us often lose the ground we once had. But we force ourselves to stand up again, dig our toes into the rock-strewn watery river bottom, and trudge on once again toward our far-distant destination. It is near impossible to stay in one spot for very long. We are either slowly, relentlessly pushing forward or being bulldozed backward by the flood.

It's my opinion that God doesn't necessarily judge us on the distance we've traveled in the river so much as which direction we are headed. I believe He would much rather have a humble daughter that is downstream a ways but pushing with all her might to get further along the path than a daughter who has already made it a little further up the watery path but has grown complacent in her efforts and is facing the wrong direction, taking her eyes off the far-distant mark.

The best news is that our Father in Heaven has not left us to trek the distraught river alone. No way! It is beyond all human capability to make the journey upstream on our own. He has thrown us a life-preserver, and as long as we hold on to it with all our might and press forward with faith in His divine assistance, we will eventually make it to our glorious destination.

Sister Patricia Holland told about an experience she had while visiting Jerusalem after an extremely difficult and trying time in her life. "On a pristinely clear and beautifully bright day, I sat overlooking the Sea of Galilee and reread the tenth chapter of Luke. I thought I saw with my mind and heard with my heart these words: '[Pat, Pat, Pat], thou art careful and troubled about many things.'" Sister Holland said that as she sat pondering her numerous problems, she felt the sun's healing rays, "like warm liquid pouring into my heart—relaxing, calming, and comforting my troubled soul." She continued, "Our loving Father in Heaven seemed to be whispering to me, 'You don't have to worry over so many things. The one thing that is needful, the only thing that is truly needful—is to keep your eyes toward the sun—my Son.'"[5]

Brother Robinson observed, "The weight of the demand for perfection has driven [many women] to despair. They mistakenly feel that in order for the Atonement to work in their lives, they must first become perfect through their own efforts. But anyone who could meet this requirement would not need the Atonement at all, for such a person would already be reconciled to God, having achieved the celestial standard of perfection on his or her own without needing Christ and His atonement—and this is not possible."[6]

He then stated, "Thus the most important goal in mortality is becoming one with Christ through the gospel covenant and gaining access through that union to *His* perfection, rather than remaining separate and aloof while trying (fruitlessly!) to generate our own perfection and thereby save ourselves."[7]

This is the "good news" of the gospel. We do not need to face this mortal journey on our own. In fact, we cannot face this mortal journey on our own if we desire to make it to our ultimate destination of becoming one with God, becoming perfect like He is. So keep your eyes on His Son, push forward with faith, and be patient with yourself. And you will one day become perfected in Him.

REFERENCES

1. Patricia Holland, "One Thing Needful: Becoming Women of Greater Faith in Christ," *Ensign*, October 1987.
2. Ibid.
3. Stephen E. Robinson, *Believing Christ*, (Salt Lake City: Deseret Book, 1992), 15–16.
4. Dieter F. Uchtdorf, "Forget Me Not," *Ensign*, November 2011
5. Patricia Holland, "One Thing Needful: Becoming Women of Greater Faith in Christ," *Ensign*, October 1987.
6. Stephen E. Robinson, *Believing Christ*, (Salt Lake City: Deseret Book, 1992), 13.
7. Ibid., 14; italics added.

CLEANING

MOMS WHO CLEAN HOUSE

"If today you are a little better than you were
yesterday, then that's good enough."
—DAVID A. BEDNAR[1]

President Monson once stated that, "Our task is to become our best selves."[2] We know that we cannot become completely perfect in this life—it's impossible. We can, however, work to improve ourselves while on this mortal journey. Jeffery R. Holland stated something that I truly believe when he said, "God doesn't care nearly as much about where you have been as He does about where you are and, with His help, where you are willing to go."[3] How then do we go about becoming better mothers, better wives, and better disciples of God, as President Monson suggested we do?

How many women, when cleaning their homes, race around from dirty room to dirty room trying to clean the whole of their house all at once? Cleaning out their closets while simultaneously running over to mop their bathroom floors. Washing their dirty dishes while at the same time trying to vacuum their dust-filled carpets. That doesn't sound like a very practical or effective way to clean, if you ask me! Not only would I be tired out within ten minutes of racing back and forth throughout my house, but I'd also feel overwhelmed and soon want to give up. On the upside though, I would probably lose a few pounds, which would be nice, but that's beside the point!

The best way I've learned to clean my messy house is by focusing on one task at a time. If I see that dirty dishes are overflowing out of my sink and a foul odor is starting to emanate from over in that direction—they are what I'll choose to focus on first. They are the most urgent disaster. I grab my scouring pad and a gas mask and scrub away at the dishes until they are sparkling clean. Phew! That's one check off my massive list! Next, I'll move on to the next most urgent mess in my house. "Wow! I wonder when the last time was that I took out the trash!" I'm smelling something pretty gnarly coming from that direction as well. I throw the gas mask back on, along with some yellow rubber gloves, and out goes our rotting trash. There! Another check off my list. Yay, I'm feeling pretty good about myself right now! Let's see . . . what do I want to check off my list next? Hmmm . . . maybe the laundry, considering my kids have been wearing the same outfits for almost a week now! I'll get right on that. It's a little bit of a longer process but that's alright; it's important that I get it done. I finally finish my laundry and can now check it off my list too. I'm on a roll!

The methodical and calculated process of focusing on one bad aspect of my house and working on it until it's nice and clean and then moving on to my next dirty job has worked out great for me *and* my house. It doesn't have me overwhelmed, since I'm concentrating all my efforts on only one single task. It doesn't wear me out too much because I'm not running back and forth throughout my house. And the best part is that I'm continually seeing progress, slow though it may be, which pumps me up and makes me want to continue on to achieve my goal of a clean house. It's hard work. But it needs to get done, so I'll do it. I know I'll feel much happier and more relaxed hanging out in my house after all the grime and nasty smells are gone and it's become nice and clean.

Similarly, we all have spiritual imperfections and weaknesses that make us unclean in the eyes of God. I guess you can say that our spiritual houses need a tidying up. We don't need to feel bad or guilty about this; it's just a fact of life and a law of nature. Entropy is the physical degradation of things that are organized. Clean rooms turn into dirty rooms. Clean clothes turn into dirty clothes. And organized matter in the form of planets come into and go out of existence. This same principle of entropy applies to spiritual things as well. In all cases, Satan and the natural forces of this universe are trying to wear us down, break us down, and keep us down until we've been diminished into nothing.

Ridding ourselves of the natural man within us and becoming "new creatures" (2 Corinthians 5:17) in Christ sounds like a daunting task. But that's precisely why we're in this mortal existence— to learn how to overcome these weaknesses, and with Christ's assistance, work on them until they become strengths. The first step in this critical process is recognizing our weaknesses. We can't clean something we don't know needs cleaning! Are we too judgmental? Do we get offended too easily? Are we impatient? Are we focused too much on worldly possessions or worldliness? Do we watch or listen to media that we know is bad for our spiritual growth? Are we lackadaisical in our prayers or our scripture study habits? Do we need to be better at attending the temple? This list is just a minuscule sampling of the many different weaknesses each of us have to deal with on a daily basis. And guess what . . . it's alright! You're alright! We just need to get to work cleaning these areas of our nature.

Often we see the numerous areas of our lives that need disinfecting and we start to feel completely overwhelmed. We don't know how or where to begin. We know these areas need to be spruced up a little (or a lot), but working on all of our weaknesses simultaneously wears out even the best of us! We begin to feel dejected and disheartened because it seems as though we're making little progress. We can't see the end in sight so we end up talking ourselves out of putting in our full effort and instead slide by, doing a half-hearted job—telling ourselves that it's good enough.

Instead of the "all at once" approach, we should focus on one aspect of our lives that needs improving at a time, just like we use when cleaning our homes. It's the "cleaning house" approach. Focus on just one weakness, that's it! Clean it up, and move on to the next. For example, if you need to improve upon your daily personal scripture study, set a goal that you will read your scriptures every day at such and such a time for the next 30 days. Call it your 30-day challenge. My kids love these challenges. Hang a sticky note up on your bathroom mirror if it will help you remember to meet your goal each day. For the next 30 days, make that single area of improvement one of the main focuses of your day. Hang up a chart that you can mark off each day after you have fulfilled it. This will help you to feel a sense of accomplishment each day and motivate you to continue. It may take one month or longer to form this habit, but if you are putting all your focus and willpower towards accomplishing this one goal for a set amount of time, it should be able to stick and become a part of you. When this has become a habit for you, when it's no longer a challenge but is part of your everyday routine . . . move on to the next mess. Set a goal and follow the same process. But make sure to continue on with the goal you have already met! If the first goal is still a real challenge for you, hold back from moving on until it becomes easier. You don't want to overwhelm yourself or you may end up feeling like a failure—and that would not be good for your psyche. If it takes you a whole year to truly have it become a habit, so be it. Time is not the important thing. Improving that aspect of your life is what's important.

The prophet Jacob spoke about this process of "cleaning house" when he was giving his allegory of the tame and wild olive trees. "Ye shall clear away the bad according as the good shall grow, that the root and the top may be equal in strength, until the good shall overcome the bad, and the bad be hewn down and cast into the fire, that they cumber not the ground of my vineyard; and thus will I sweep away the bad out of my vineyard" (Jacob 5:66).

Further, when cleaning, do we simply use our hands to do all the wiping, washing, and disinfecting? Do we walk around dusting our furniture with the palms of our hands? Do we swing our family's clothes around with our hands in hopes that the dirt just magically flies right off of them? Do we hold up our dishes and lick them clean in order to sterilize them? Eww, gross! Of course not! Without the proper tools, no matter what effort we put into cleaning our house, the stains and germs will still remain. The tools are what truly enable us to clean and disinfect properly. So, instead of dusting with the palms of our hands, we use a nice clean cloth to catch all the dust and dirt. We use water and detergent and then scrub vigorously to enable the grimy dirt to come off of our clothes. Again, we use hot water and soap to clean the crusty food off our dishes and to kill the destructive germs that may be lingering.

We know that there is absolutely no possible way that we can save ourselves and become clean and perfected on our own. That's the Savior's gift to us. But we also know that our faithful and obedient actions to God's commandments show our Heavenly Father that we are willing to accept His divine gift in our lives. As President Uchtdorf once stated, "Salvation cannot be bought with the currency of obedience; it is purchased by the blood of the Son of God. . . . Grace is a gift of God, and our desire to be obedient to each of God's commandments is the reaching out of our mortal hand to receive this sacred gift from our Heavenly Father."[4]

Christ's single greatest mission was to take disorganized and decayed physical and spiritual things and make them clean and whole again. His role was to bring the disinfecting power of the Atonement into a dirty house, so to speak. He conjured this power through the act of the Atonement. This is the single greatest tool God has given his children to help us clean house. God sent down his Son to fulfill the Atonement for the precise purpose of giving us both a cleaning agent—the cleansing power of the Atonement which "disinfects" us. And through the enabling power of the Atonement, we gain the *strength* to go on when otherwise we could not; we gain power *beyond* our own strength or ability. It was hard work for Christ fulfilling His mission and so we can expect for it to be hard for us.

The power to fully cleanse our inner vessel is within reach of us all . . . if we will call upon that power. God will not only help us conquer our many weaknesses but He will actually turn them into strengths if we allow Him to work in our lives. "For if they humble themselves before me, and have faith in me, then will I make weak things become strong unto them" (Ether 12:27). This is how God works in the lives of His children who humbly ask for His divine assistance. God fills us with His mighty power and then we use His power to become better and more faithful children.

As our children see us slowly and methodically working to improve ourselves daily, they will learn the habits of self-improvement as we set the example for them. They will learn that by partnering with the Lord, they will be able to become more than they ever knew or dreamed they could be. "The Lord works from the inside out, the world works from the outside in. The world would take the people out of the slums. Christ takes the slums out of the people, and then they take themselves out of the slums. The world would mold men by changing their environment. Christ changes men, who then change their environment. The world would shape human behavior, but Christ can change human nature."[5]

REFERENCES

1.   David A Bednar, as quoted by Mormon Channel, Facebook, August 9, 2013, https://www.facebook.com/pg/mormonchannel/posts.
2.   Thomas S. Monson, "The Will Within," *Ensign*, May 1987.
3.   Jeffrey R. Holland, "The Best Is Yet to Be," *Ensign*, January 2010.
4.   Dieter F. Uchtdorf, "The Gift of Grace," *Ensign*, May 2015.
5.   Ezra Taft Benson, "Born of God," *Ensign*, July 1989.

You are
NOT
alone in this.

GOD
is
with you.

MOMS WHO FEEL ALONE

"Though it may seem that you are alone, angels attend you. Though you may feel that no one can understand the depth of your despair, our Savior, Jesus Christ, understands. He suffered more than we can possibly imagine, and he did it for us; He did it for you. You are not alone."
—DIETER F. UCHTDORF[1]

Most of us have had times where we have felt completely and utterly alone in this life. No matter how many people we were surrounded by throughout the day—our husbands, kids, neighbors, friends, co-workers—we still felt totally alone. These feelings of complete loneliness may be brought on by family calamities, such as the death of a loved one or divorce. They may be brought on by personal sorrows that weigh us down and feel too heavy for us to bear alone. They may be brought on by the mental anguish of sin, or the intense pain of illness. Or by a number of other distressing occurrences that come with the territory of being a part of this mortal journey.

During these times, we may feel like God, too, has abandoned us for some reason. Maybe we feel like we are not special enough or worthy enough for Him to show us His hands working in our lives. Maybe we feel like our lives are too insignificant for the God of all to set His gaze upon us. After a while, we may begin to feel like maybe His hands actually aren't working in our lives at all. We have faith, we believe that God is there, but maybe He's just not there for us. We plead for God to reveal Himself. To show us some sign that we are loved by Him and that He is working for our good, somehow, in some way not fully disclosed to us at the moment.

These periods of loneliness and perceived abandonment can make us feel as though our worth in the eyes of our Heavenly Father is infinitesimal, and, by extension, our worth in our own eyes dwindles immensely. We are left feeling hopeless, as though we are in a pitch-black room with no sense of where the door to escape is located. So we are left kneeling on our hands and knees—feeling, grasping for anything, any sign that will indicate to us that the way to escape this bitter darkness is near. We pray and beg for our Savior to come and save us from our debilitating grief.

I remember almost like it was yesterday the night I was watching the news and glimpsed the photo of the evil and disgusting man the police were searching for in relation to the kidnapping of Elizabeth Smart. I was with Greg at his house, watching the news with his family. When the news channel put up the photo of the man they were searching for, Greg and I gaped at each other in utter disbelief.

Just a few months earlier, in the month of August to be exact, Greg and I, along with Greg's best friend, Brian, left California to drive up to Salt Lake to visit the temple. Little did I know the real purpose for the trip. Greg was planning to propose to me there while walking the temple grounds. His friend's purpose, unbeknownst to me, was to act as videographer, hiding in the greenery around the great stone edifice.

Back in Greg's living room, as we sat there watching the television in shock and horror, we saw pictured on the news the same man we had emptied our wallets for the night of our engagement at the temple in Salt Lake. This disgusting man was sitting outside the great stone walls panhandling in his long dingy white robes and stringy brown hair. We felt sorry for the man. I remember Greg and I saying to each other that either this man was a total psychopath or one of those angels that you could be entertaining unawares at any moment, as it mentions in the scriptures. You shouldn't judge us too harshly, after all, we were young, and he was dressed up as a holy man. Little did we know at that time just how psycho he really was. Much more than that. How evil he really was. Devilish doesn't begin to describe the depths of the blackness of this man's tar-stained soul.

Listening to Elizabeth tell her story via audiobook, my spirit cringes in horror and disbelief at the depths of ugliness and depravity she was surrounded by on every side. An innocent fourteen-year-old girl, under the constant control of two monsters. I can't imagine . . . it's impossible for me to even comprehend the loneliness and isolation she was forced to endure. Being kidnapped at knifepoint in the middle of the night. Forced to hike mile upon rocky mile into the mountains above her Salt Lake Valley home to an encampment, where she was chained like a dog on a leash for months. Being told that if she ever tried to escape, her whole family would be killed. She was starved and abused both mentally and physically for the whole nine months of her captivity. What an unthinkable nightmare that turned reality for this young and innocent daughter of God.

Where was God while all this was happening? Was He asleep? On vacation? Or maybe He just didn't think it worth His while to help one of His innocent children who was suffering in the depths of sorrow and despair. Was she alone through it all?

As I listened further to Elizabeth tell her story, it was interesting to hear her answer to that very question. She starts by quoting two lines from a sacred hymn:

> *The pains of all of them he carried.*
> *From the day of His birth.*[2]

How does our Savior carry all the pains and sorrows of us all? She continues:

> Are their pains eliminated? Are they saved from all suffering? In some cases they aren't, at least not in this world. Yet if their pains are not eliminated, how then are they comforted? How are their burdens lifted? How are their pains carried? I don't have all the answers. But this much I know. Sometimes there are miracles—'tender mercies' some have called them—that comfort us in ways that other people may not see. Sometimes things are offered that we may not know about. Things that give those who suffer strength. Things that give them hope. Things that help them

to hang on. That certainly was the case for me. I felt some of these miracles along the way.[3]

Elizabeth goes on to describe the first miracle she received from God during her enslavement. She said that a few days before her kidnapping, her Grandpa Francon, whom she was very close to, passed away. He had been extremely active and healthy, but shortly before Elizabeth's bondage, doctors found a large tumor in his brain. His funeral was the day before her nightmare began.

She describes:

> God knew what was about to happen to me. I think that's why He brought my grandpa home. He knew that Grandpa Francon could be more helpful to me from the other side of the veil. Grandpa was one of my guardian angels. He was sent to comfort and inspire me in the very darkest hours, to help me find reasons for hope or encouragement when I felt the most despair. There were many occasions during the time that I was captured when I felt his spirit near.
>
> During the darkest days that I was captive, it helped me to think that someone I loved, someone who loved me, someone who was a good man, was standing by my side. It helped me remember that God still cared for me, that He hadn't forgotten or forsaken me, that he was doing everything He could to help to carry my pain. It brought me comfort to think that Grandpa was helping me too, giving me a little strength when I had nowhere else to turn, nothing else to hope for, nothing in my life but pain and fear. Yes, I believe that God helped to carry me. In fact, I know that He did.[4]

Throughout her book, Elizabeth lists a number of miracles that occurred throughout the nine excruciating months of her imprisonment. Some large, some simple, but each one of them profound. For instance, there was a time early on in her captivity that she had to go without water for a number of days.

"It was the middle of June, deep into the boiling days of summer. Utah is a desert and it had not rained since the first week that I was captured. Temperatures hovered in the nineties, sometimes reaching above a hundred. A hot wind blew every afternoon, drying us like leather. My skin was dry, my throat, my eyes. I was so dirty and so thirsty that I thought I would die."[5]

Elizabeth describes how one night, after she had finally fallen into a restless sleep, she was suddenly awakened in the middle of the night. To her great astonishment, Elizabeth found, sitting next to her pillow, an ice-cold cup of water, full to the brim. Wondering if she was dreaming or delusional, she picked up the cup and drank from it. "The water cooled my throat and filled my stomach. It was cold and clear and wonderful, the best-tasting water that I had ever had."[6]

Of this experience she explained:

> Why did God do it? How did it happen? What was God trying to say? Would I have died without the water? Certainly not. As thirsty as I felt, as terrible as it was, I was not teetering on the edge of a life-or-death situation. . . . So why did God send me the water? Because He loved me. And He wanted me to know. He wanted me to know that He was still near. He wanted me to know that He controlled the Earth and all the heavens, that all things were in His hands. And if He could move mountains, then he could do this thing for me. To Him it was a small thing—a terribly easy thing to do—but for me it was as powerful as if He had parted the sea. . . . This experience reminded me once again that God had not deserted me, that He was aware of my suffering and loneliness. And that assurance gave me hope. It helped me to keep my faith and gave me the strength that I needed to go on.[7]

Elizabeth had many more miraculous experiences during her time in confinement. Most of them were simple yet penetrating messages of comfort and hope, whispered to her mind, that gave her the strength to go on.

Speaking of her experiences she concluded, "I think there are far more miracles in our lives than we may ever realize. Like flickers of light among the darkness, they remind us that God is there and that He cares."[8]

Although Elizabeth had unimaginable trauma occur for nine months out of her life, her own mother, Lois, was another one of these God-sent angels that helped her get through this nightmare. Elizabeth explained that on the day of her rescue, her mother pulled her off to one side and gave her the best piece of advice that she will always remember and incorporate into her life.

Her mom advised, "Elizabeth . . . don't you let him steal one more second of your life. Not one more second! You be happy. *You move on.*"[9]

Because of this angelic advice from her loving mother, Elizabeth was able to move forward with her life and not let these past horrific experiences destroy her future.

Elizabeth is now a mother of her own and can truly testify to her children that she knows—she knows—that God hears every whisper, every plea for help, every call for rescue that each and every one of His precious children cries out for. She knows He's there because she grew to know Him throughout her struggles.

So many of us, in our own personal loneliness, cry out to God to hear our plea. To comfort us in some way shape or form. This was true of one of my pioneer ancestors who crossed the plains with the Saints during those trying early years of the Church. Her name was Amanda Barnes Smith and was a victim in the ill-fated Haun's Mill massacre. From Amanda's journal, I learned that during that horrendous ordeal, her husband, Warren, and her ten-year-old son, Sardius, were both brutally murdered by a ruthless mob of 300 men, simply because of their fervent faith in the restored gospel of Jesus Christ. Amanda's six-year-old son, Alma, "had his hip shot off, the entire hip joint and socket gone."[10]

Shortly after the massacre, the vicious mob members threatened the remaining women with their lives if they were ever heard crying out to God in prayer. My grandmother wrote in her journal: "I could bear it no longer. I pined to hear once more my own voice in petition to my Heavenly Father."

She quickly stole down and hid herself in a lush corn field. She describes:

> I prayed aloud most fervently. When I emerged from the corn, a voice spoke to me. It was a voice as plain as I ever heard one. It was no silent, strong impression of the spirit, but a voice, repeating a verse of the saint's hymn:
> "*That soul who on Jesus hath leaned for repose,*
> *I cannot, I will not desert to its foes;*

That soul, though all hell should endeavor to shake,
I'll never, no never, no never forsake!"

From that moment on, I had no more fear. I felt like nothing could hurt me.[11]

After the devastating murder of her husband and ten-year-old son, Amanda was left to tend to her six-year-old son, Alma, who had his hip shot away while hiding in the Blacksmith shop.

She explained, "The entire hip joint of my wounded boy had been shot away. Flesh, hip bone, joint and all had been ploughed out from the muzzle of the gun, which the ruffian placed to the child's hip through the logs of the shop and deliberately fired. We laid little Alma on a bed in our tent and I examined the wound. It was a ghastly sight. *I knew not what to do.*"

Amanda, in desperation, pled with the Lord, "Oh my Heavenly Father, what shall I do? Thou sees my poor wounded boy and knows my inexperience. Oh Heavenly Father, direct me what to do! *And then I was directed as by a voice speaking to me.*"

She says, "The ashes of our fire were still smoldering. We had been burning the bark of a hickory. I was directed to take those ashes and make a lye and put a cloth saturated with it right into the wound. It hurt, but Alma was too near dead to heed it much. Again and again I saturated the cloth and put it into the hole from which the hip joint had been ploughed, and each time mashed flesh and splinters of bone came away with the cloth; and the wound became as white as chicken's flesh."

She continued, "Having done as directed I again prayed to the Lord and was again instructed as distinctly as though a physician had been standing by speaking to me. Nearby was an elm tree. From this I was told to make an elm poultice and fill the wound with it.

Later the next day, when Alma finally regained consciousness, Amanda spoke to him asking:

"Alma, my child, you believe that the Lord made your hip?"

"Yes, mother."

"Well, the Lord can make something there in the place of your hip. Don't you believe he can, Alma?"

"Do you think that the Lord can, Mother?" inquired the child in his simplicity.

"Yes, my son, He has showed it all to me in a vision."

27

Continuing, she explained, "Then I laid him comfortably on his face, and said: 'Now you lay like that, and don't move, and the Lord will make you another hip.' So Alma laid on his face for five weeks, until he was entirely recovered.

News of this amazing miracle spread far and wide. Five physicians were sent by the board of doctors in St. Louis who heard of the case and desired to investigate it further to learn for themselves the truthfulness in this grandiose claim.

"After watching the action of the hip as he walked, they declared it a complete mystery. They could not understand what kind of combination it was that supplied strength and action, for the bone was gone. A sort of gristle had partly supplied the place and it was just as strong as the other leg and as active though there was a depression easily detected through his clothing."

The doctors in total amazement asked the name of the surgeon who performed this miraculous piece of surgery.

Amanda stated, "Jesus Christ."

They inquired, "Not the Savior of the world?"

She responded, "Yes, the same sir. He was the Physician and I was the nurse."[12]

My grandmother cried out to God in deep desperation. She needed the assistance that only her Father in Heaven could give to save the life of her little boy. Amanda's desperate plea was answered, and powerfully so. This horrific experience was the catalyst in bringing her the certain knowledge that God is always present in the lives of His children . . . especially during the times of greatest trial and anguish.

Life is but a Weaving—a poem often attributed to Corrie ten Boom, who, along with her family, helped to save nearly 800 Jews from extermination during the Nazi Holocaust—expresses the belief that God uses both the good times and dark times in our lives to build us into the people He sees we can become. God is there, even through the hard times, working everything for our eventual good.

My life is but a weaving
Between my God and me.
I cannot choose the colors
He weaveth steadily.
Oft' times He weaveth sorrow;
And I in foolish pride

Forget He sees the upper
And I the underside.
Not 'til the loom is silent
And the shuttles cease to fly
Will God unroll the canvas
And reveal the reason why.
The dark threads are as needful
In the weaver's skillful hand
As the threads of gold and silver
In the pattern he has planned.
He knows, He loves, He cares;
Nothing this truth can dim.
He gives the very best to those
Who leave the choice to Him.[13]

Elder Holland informs us, "Trumpeted from the summit of Calvary is the truth that we will never be left alone nor unaided, even if sometimes we may feel that we are." Further he continues, "Because Jesus walked such a long, lonely path utterly alone, we do not have to."[14]

We learn from Alma that Christ "shall go forth, suffering pains and afflictions and temptations of every kind; and this that the word might be fulfilled which saith he will take upon him the pains and the sicknesses of his people. And he will take upon him death which bind his people; and he will take upon him their infirmities, that his bowels may be filled with mercy, according to the flesh, that he may know according to the flesh, how to succor his people according to their infirmities" (Alma 7:11–12). Even our dear Savior, in His darkest of hours, felt the agony of complete abandonment. So much so, that He cried out to His Father, "My God, my God, why hast thou forsaken me?" (Matthew 27:26). This misery Jesus willingly endured for each of us in order that He might gain a perfect understanding of how to comfort us in our periods of deepest loneliness and grief.

God is aware of each one of his children. None of us need feel alone in this life—ever! No matter how old, no matter how young. No matter how difficult our circumstance. He is continually working behind the scenes in our lives for our benefit. No matter how lonely we are, no matter how insignificant we feel, no matter how unworthy we perceive ourselves being, God knows the righteous desires of our hearts and prepares a way for them to be fulfilled. Everything that God orchestrates in our lives will be revealed at some future date and we will finally be able to see that God was with us continually throughout our lives, through both the happy times and the most painful of times. Our kind Savior promises, "I will not leave you comfortless: My Father and I will come to you and abide with you (John 14:18; see also v. 23).

REFERENCES

1. Dieter F. Uchtdorf, "Your Happily Ever After," *Ensign*, May 2010.
2. Elizabeth Smart, *My Story* (New York: St. Martin's Griffin, 2013), 54.
3. Ibid. 54
4. Ibid., 55–57.
5. Ibid., 131–132.
6. Ibid.
7. Ibid.
8. Ibid., 53.
9. Ibid., 294.
10. Edward W. Tullidge, *The Women of Mormondom* (New York, 1877), 116–132.
11. Ibid.
12. Stories of Faith—The Early Mormon Saints and Pioneers: A Miracle at Haun's Mill—A Boy is Healed: David Kenison, 8-25-14 http://earlymormonsaints.blogspot.com/2014/08/a-miracle-at-hauns-mill-boy-is-healed.html?m=1
13. "Life Is But a Weaving." Unattributed.
14. Jeffery R. Holland, "None Were with Him," *Ensign*, May 2009.

MOMS WHO ARE COMPETITIVE

"If you burn your neighbor's house down, it doesn't
make your house look any better."
—LOU HOLTZ[1]

Meg Meeker, an American pediatrician and author, wrote of an experience she had over twenty years ago while driving to Children's Hospital in Milwaukee, Wisconsin, where she worked as a senior pediatric resident. Her experience began in the early morning hours, as she coasted along the lonely highway on her way to begin a grueling day at work. Meg relates how she was peacefully driving along the highway, in no rush to get to work, enjoying the serenity of her early morning commute. When all of a sudden, out of her peripheral vision, she spotted a car driving in the left-hand lane, quickly trying to pass her up. She recognized that the car belonged to a female colleague of hers who must have been on her way to make rounds at the hospital. Immediately and without even thinking, Meg's right foot reacted and her accelerator pedal was floored, she was now flying down the highway. There was no way Meg was going to let *this woman* beat her to work! The funny thing is that as soon as Meg sped up, guess who also sped up? Yep . . . the other woman! She must have been thinking the same exact thing as Meg.

She continued:

> The most peculiar part of the exchange is that neither of us
> would acknowledge the other's presence. Each time I sped up, I

pretended not to notice that she was trying to pass me. And she did the same to me. We women are clever at pretending not to notice the most obviously ridiculous things. After nine miles of cat and mouse, we flew our cars into the parking garage, hustled through the emergency room (still not acknowledging that we were racing), and made it to our respective hospital floors. I had to show her and myself that I was more on top of my game than she was, and vice versa. After all these years, neither of us will admit what we did (at least to each other). How ridiculous can two grown women be? Very ridiculous, because that is what competition brings out in us.[2]

What makes us women feel the need to compete with each other? What was it that drove Dr. Meeker to feel the compulsion to bear down on that accelerator as she raced down the deserted highway *only* once she saw a woman colleague driving next to her? Her candid answer speaks truth about our human natures—so is worth repeating, *"I had to show her and myself that I was more on top of my game than she was."* The inarguable answer is pride, which is, by definition, "a high or inordinate opinion of one's own dignity, importance, merit, or superiority."[3] The need to prove that she was better or more superior than her colleague is what drove her to race that day. Unfortunately, she's not alone in this human failing.

The sad truth is that it's within our very natures, both women and men, to be competitive. From the very beginnings of the human race, in fact, we see this ungodly trait rear its ugly head when we read the somber story of Cain and Abel. Cain was viciously jealous of his brother's flocks and lusted after them, desiring to have them for himself. So, giving in to his traitorous feelings of jealously and greed, two main components of competition, Cain ruthlessly killed his brother Abel, and set his path on the descending road toward destruction.

Even from before the foundations of the world, we see how Satan's prideful competitive nature proved his everlasting downfall when, "In the pre-earthly council, Lucifer placed his proposal in competition with the Father's plan as advocated by Jesus Christ. He wished to be honored above all others. In short, his prideful desire was to dethrone God." In other words, "In the premortal council, it was pride that felled Lucifer, 'a son of the morning.'"[4]

The Book of Mormon is a record of a once great but fallen people. What was the source of their fall? The prophet Mormon tells us, "Behold, the *pride* of this nation, or the people of the Nephites, hath proven their destruction" (Moroni 8:27). The Doctrine and Covenants blatantly warns us who live in the latter days, "Beware of pride, lest ye become as the Nephites of old" (D&C 38:39). We can search through every book of scripture as well as every history textbook and read account after account of how pride destroyed individual people, families, and nations.

Speaking of this base aspect of our nature, Ezra Taft Benson stated, "Pride is essentially competitive in nature. . . . The proud make every man their adversary by pitting their intellects, opinions, works, wealth, talents, or any other worldly measuring device against others." He continues by quoting the great C. S. Lewis, "Pride gets no pleasure out of having something, only out of having more of it than the next man. It is the comparison that makes you proud: the pleasure of being above the rest. Once the element of competition has gone, pride has gone."[5]

Dieter F. Uchtdorf distinguishes:

> I believe there is a difference between being proud of certain things and being prideful. I am proud of many things. I am proud of my wife. I am proud of our children and grandchildren. . . . So what's the difference between this kind of feeling and the pride that President Benson called 'the universal sin'? Pride is sinful because it breeds hatred or hostility and places us in opposition to God and our fellowmen. At its core, pride is a sin of comparison, for though it usually begins with 'Look how wonderful I am and what great things I have done,' it always seems to end with 'Therefore, I am better than you.'[6]

Satan has an absolute field day with this aspect of our natures. Working to turn the children of God *against* each other in competition rather than *towards* each other in compassion as our loving Heavenly Father would have us do. From the very earliest moments of our journey here in mortality, competition has been a part of our daily lives. It has become ingrained in who we are as human beings. We are literally surrounded by it.

Think about the billions upon billions of dollars and time spent annually on competition. Think about all the televised sporting events and sports gear purchased which purposefully pit one team against another. Think about how much money is spent between competing political rivals during election season. What about all the highly profitable reality shows and highly competitive song and dance shows whose whole premise is to eliminate those competitors who aren't "as good" until one rises up out of the masses as not only the grand-prize winner, but also as the next "star" to be idolized.

And what about all the marketing ads whose sole purpose is to make us feel like we need this item or that item in order to look *more* attractive or *more* successful than those of our peers. Work promotions are focused on competition. And sadly, even some feel competitive when it comes to our church callings. Our children's schools are all focused on competition from early grammar school all the way up through college admissions and beyond.

And don't even get me started on how insane some parents get when it comes to the competitive aspects of their kids' sports teams! My children recently attended their cousin's soccer game, where they had to witness a mom of one of the players being forced to leave the premises for unruly conduct. This was no high school championship game or anything, my nephew is nine. His teammates are all in grade school. Can you say *crazy*?! A nice and loving parent can instantaneously turn into the mindless Hulk if their child is taken out of "the big game" and replaced with someone else's kid. "How dare they! My child is twice the player so-and-so's child is!" All the while their child is sitting on the bench, ears open wide, listening and learning through the sorry example of the parent.

Dr. Meeker explains how this debilitating sin affects us women most commonly, "Every one of us mothers competes with other mothers in some way. The biggest difficulty with the game is that it is usually disguised and deeply hidden from even our own sight. And most of us would never admit that we do it. But if we really want to live healthier, happier lives, we've got to call ourselves out on it." She continues, "We look [at a woman's] appearance and we make quick judgements in our minds about it. If she is out of shape or overweight, we may feel better about ourselves. But if she has a lovely figure, we feel a twinge of envy. We do this not because we're bad people, but because that's what we're trained to do—size women up."[7] It's what the media, along with their marketing agencies, teach us to do from the earliest of ages. They decide for the world what should be considered beautiful and enviable, and they make every woman within the sound of their ad believe they need that product in order to be happy.

Even beyond our looks, as women, it seems as though we compare everything to that of our female peers. And we either feel pride over seemingly having more than they do or feel less worthy for seemingly having less than they do. We compare our houses, careers, financial status, clothes, talents, education, achievements of our children . . . you name it, we compare it. And we feel either the pride of victory over them or dejection at the undesirable outcome.

Ezra Taft Benson said, "Pride is a sin that can readily be seen in others but is rarely admitted in ourselves. Most of us consider pride to be a sin of those on the top, such as the rich and the learned, looking down at the rest of us. There is, however, a far more common ailment among us—and that is pride from the bottom looking up. It is manifest in so many ways, such as faultfinding, gossiping, backbiting, murmuring, living beyond our means, envying, coveting, withholding gratitude and praise that might lift another, and being unforgiving and jealous."[8]

President Uchtdorf expanded upon this thought when he stated, "For others, pride turns to envy: they look bitterly at those who have better positions, more talents, or greater possessions than they do. They seek to hurt, diminish, and tear down others in a misguided and unworthy attempt at self-elevation. When those they envy stumble or suffer, they secretly cheer."[9]

Pride is the parent of all other sins we will commit in this earthly realm. All other sins are just appendages attached to the great sin of pride. Think about it: what sin is there that doesn't first begin with us inserting our wants and desires above that of another person . . . or even above God? None that I can think of! Prideful competition is the ultimate Satanic attribute, while loving compassion is the ultimate Christlike attribute. They are the polar opposites of each other. We cannot hope to become Christlike without first working to root out the poison of pride and competition from within ourselves.

So how do we overcome this fatal flaw in our natures?

Well, the first step in overcoming any addiction, including the addiction of comparison, is to recognize when we are doing it! We can't fix something we don't recognize or admit to. It may have become so natural that we don't even think twice about it. Consciously examine your thoughts as you go out into your daily life. Notice when you are having unwarranted harsh or judgmental feelings towards another woman, or towards yourself for that matter. When we understand the ramifications of continuing down this dead-end course, we can start to make course corrections and choose to go down the higher road that Christ walked down.

The second step is to work on controlling our thoughts. As James Allen once said, "A man is literally what he thinks, his character being the complete sum of all his thoughts. As a plant springs from, and could not be without, the seed, so every act of a man springs from the hidden seeds of thought, and could not have appeared without them."[10]

My dad throughout his life has memorized countless poems and has passed that love on to me. The kids in my family all knew that at least once a day we would hear a poem fall from his lips along with the follow up question of "what's the meaning behind it?" I once asked my dad why he got so interested in memorizing poems. His answer surprised me. I wasn't expecting it at all! He informed me that he started memorizing poems in his adolescent years in order to help himself control his thoughts while he went throughout his day. While he was at work, at the gym, or wherever he went, if an unworthy thought popped into his head, he would repeat a poem to himself in order to change the focus of his mind.

Similarly, I've heard Elder Bednar and others talk about reciting church hymns in their minds if an unclean thought enters their mind.[11] I've heard this tip in the past pointed more towards those of the male gender who are struggling to keep their thoughts clean and pure, but it would surely work for us women just as well. If an unkind thought pops in your head, quickly refocus your mind on something else such as a memorized poem, hymn, scripture . . . or even on your grocery list, just so long as it helps you reroute your thoughts in a different and more uplifting direction.

The third step I suggest would be to create a list of things about your life that you're grateful for. Whether you write down in your journal each day some things that you recognize as being blessings in your life, or whether you simply list them in your head as you go about your day, I believe this effort will help you to center your mind on the positive aspects of your life rather than on the negative. Much of our jealousy and envy comes though focusing our minds on the things we are lacking rather than on the things that we have been blessed with.

Gordon B. Hinckley informs us, "Generally speaking, the most miserable people I know are those who are obsessed with themselves. By and large, if we complain about life, it is because we are thinking only of ourselves." He continues, "For many years, there was a sign on the wall of a shoe shop I patronized that read: 'I complained because I had no shoes until I saw a man who had no feet.' The most effective medicine for the sickness of self-pity is to lose ourselves in the service of others who may not have as much as we do."[12]

And this brings us to our fourth and final step. Dr. Meeker explains:

> One of the best ways I know to ward off jealousy is to speak well of the woman who has something we want. This is akin to praying for our enemies, if you will, and it is really tough to do. The more competitive we feel with another mom, the more we subconsciously dislike her and the harder it is not to criticize her, let alone say nice things about her. But this is exactly what we must do. And, after a while, it feels good. Giving praise to someone you have hard feelings for—particularly when you do it sincerely and to her face—heals all sorts of ills. It is remarkable. . . . Saying nice things, praising other mothers, and encouraging one another whenever possible changes us. Jealousy goes away and relationships grow.[13]

I know I've spoken pretty harshly on competition. I'm not trying to be the party pooper that puts the damper on the beloved BYU/U of U rivalry. I think I'd need to continually watch my back if I did that! But what I am trying to do is to help each one of us recognize within ourselves when a little bit of innocent and playful competition turns into an unhealthy and spiritually damaging version of competition.

President Uchtdorf states, "We must realize that all of God's children wear the same jersey. Our team is the brotherhood [and sisterhood] of man. This mortal life is our playing field. Our goal is to learn to love God and to extend that same love toward our fellowman. . . . We are here to build, uplift, treat fairly, and encourage all of Heavenly Father's children."[14]

The healthiest form of competition, I believe, is when we focus not on comparing ourselves with others but when we compare our today's self with our yesterday's self. That should be the true focus of our competition. Competition of this nature is what leads to progression. It's what this whole life is about. Becoming better today than we were yesterday and so on, and teaching this form of competition to our children rather than the detrimental form. As we work towards mastering our thoughts, our relationships within our families will grow, our relationships with other women will begin to blossom, and a healthy relationship with our inner selves will start to emerge. Most importantly, our eyes will be opened to all the ways we have truly been blessed by our Heavenly Father and our gratitude towards Him will grow immeasurably.

REFERENCES

1. Lou Holtz, as quoted in Dick Harmon, "Lou Holtz, ESPN Part Ways But His Quotes, Personality Will Endure," *Deseret News Sports*, April 13, 2015, https://www.deseretnews.com/article/865626320/Lou-Holtz-ESPN-part-ways-but-his-quotes-personality-will-endure.html.
2. Meg Meeker, M.D., *The 10 Habbits of Happy Mothers: Reclaiming Our Passion, Purpose, and Sanity*, (New York: Ballantine Books, 2011), 67–68.
3. Dictionary.com, *s.v.* "pride," accessed October 2017, http://www.dictionary.com/browse/pride.
4. Ezra Taft Benson, "Beware of Pride," *Ensign*, May 1989.
5. Ibid.
6. Dieter F. Uchtdorf, "Pride and the Priesthood," *Ensign*, November 2010.
7. Meg Meeker, M.D., *The 10 Habbits of Happy Mothers: Reclaiming Our Passion, Purpose, and Sanity*, (New York: Ballantine Books, 2011), 70.
8. Ezra Taft Benson, "Beware of Pride," *Ensign*, May 1989.

9. Dieter F. Uchtdorf, "Pride and the Priesthood," *Ensign*, November 2010.

10. James Allen, *As A Man Thinketh* (1903), 4.

11. David A. Bednar, "Face to Face with Elder and Sister Bednar (presentation, The Church of Jesus Christ of Latter-day Saints, Salt Lake City, UT, October 5, 2015).

12. Gordon B Hinckley, *Standing For Something: 10 Neglected Virtues That Will Heal Our Hearts and Homes* (New York: Times Books, 2000), 56.

13. Meg Meeker, M.D., *The 10 Habbits of Happy Mothers: Reclaiming Our Passion, Purpose, and Sanity*, (New York: Ballantine Books, 2011), 86–87.

14. Dieter F. Uchtdorf, "Pride and the Priesthood," *Ensign*, November 2010.

Take a
Time Out

MOMS WHO NEED A TIME OUT

"He that is slow to anger is better than the mighty; and he that ruleth his spirit than he that taketh a city."
—PROVERBS 16:32

O K, so I confess. I sometimes need to give myself a time out for bad behavior. I can't always hold myself together perfectly in certain situations. You know, like when our senile dog, Duke, who has irritable bowel syndrome, poops on the carpet for the third time in one week and then steps in it, tracking it all throughout our house. Or when my kids leave out the brand-new tubs of ice cream and they *surprisingly* melt all over the counter, leaking down onto the kitchen floor, with both children informing me that it wasn't them that left out the now liquefied dessert. Or when our garbage disposal breaks, followed by our dishwasher, followed by our air conditioner . . . literally in a row! Or when I give up my whole Saturday to clean and sanitize our home, only to have it look *exactly* how it did prior to my cleaning only a couple hours later!

Yeah . . . sometimes I feel like ripping my hair out and screaming in frustration. Other times I just sort of sit there in a catatonic stupor from shock. If I'm being honest with myself, it's not the specific situations that make it hard for me to sometimes hold it together, but it's the accumulation of occurrences such as these that make it at times feel almost impossible for me to get a grip on myself. Like when it seems that they all happen simultaneously.

I'm going to relate an experience I had a few years back that I'm fully ashamed to admit but that I think will get my point across quite nicely.

Each day before they would start the school day, my kids knew that it was their task to get their daily schedules done. This consisted of quickly picking up their bedrooms, playroom, school room, and the hallway. I'd give them an hour to get this done and they usually did a really great job of it. On this one particular morning, though, as I went about my morning chores, I detected that Taylor and Trenton were playing much more than they were actually cleaning. I reminded them numerous times of the consequences they would earn if they didn't finish their chores before it was time for school . . . but still they played on.

Each time I would come up the stairs, I would see them messing around rather than working. And I would get more and more annoyed. They were totally ignoring me! How dare they! Eventually the time came to start school and as I walked up the stairs, I couldn't believe it. The rooms looked as though nothing had been cleaned *at all*! If anything, they looked worse! Clothes strewn everywhere, toys littering the ground, the hall was still a maze of junk to clamber over. I was enraged! How could they have wasted this hour that had been given them!

Now, at this moment, I had an instantaneous choice to make. I could immediately act on my rage and run in there and scream at them, like I felt like doing. Or, I could turn around, walk into my room, shut the door, say a little prayer for peace, and then return to the scene of the crime and calmly and *unreactively* deliver the sentences they earned, the consequences affixed to their actions. I'm sure we could all say right now, without a doubt, which choice would be the more effective one. But I bet each of you can take a pretty good guess at which choice I made.

As I fiercely gazed over the hallway of destruction, the rage boiled inside my body. Even then, when the hour was up and it was time to start school, they were still playing! I couldn't believe it! I harshly grabbed the empty toy tub that was *still* lying carelessly upside-down on the hallway floor. I had asked them at least twice that morning to pick it up and put the toys back in it and yet, there it was, still there! Ooh, was I mad! Holding the neglected toy bin in my clenched fists, I chucked it back into the playroom where it belonged with all the pent-up frustration I could muster.

It's important to note at this time that my kids had within their playroom a big plastic ball pit with a slide attached to it. It's also important to note that my aim when it comes to throwing—especially if I'm angry—is not very good. With those thoughts in mind, as the giant red bin flew through the air, I could see, almost as if in slow motion, right where it was about to land. And the trajectory was *not* good! The bin landed right at the base of the slide, but instead of stopping, it kept going and slid right up the slide and crashed into the giant glass window behind it! Pieces of glass shattered everywhere. My kids quickly dashed out of the room where they had been playing, horrified at the terrible crashing sound that blasted in their ears. When they entered their playroom and saw the partially busted window, both their eyes and mouths stood agape at the scene. They stared at me in disbelief. They couldn't believe what their loving mother had just done!

Now, because I chose to be reactionary, I turned a potentially great learning experience for my kids, a time for them to receive payment for their efforts (or lack thereof), into a mess—literally and figuratively—that I needed to clean up. Instead of teaching them from the consequences of their own bad actions, the learning that day was turned to focus more on the consequences of *my* heathenistic actions.

How could this incident have been avoided? Well, I think that's pretty obvious! I should have made the other choice. I should have taken a little break or given myself a little time out when I felt my nerves starting to rub raw. I should have said a prayer to help release my anger. Then I should have walked out, calm and collected, and taught them the eternal principle of choice and accountability. Fortunately, they still ended up learning a great lesson that day, just not in the manner I had hoped.

My patriarchal blessing contains a specific paragraph that urges me to create a home where the spirit of Christ can come and I won't have to be ashamed of what has been said or done in my home. It advises me to be kind and considerate to my family and to express love *always*. It encourages me to be fully committed to this goal and to make it permeate everything I do, for the responsibility of raising a righteous family is the most important responsibility I can have.

Well, I definitely had a major fail *that* day!

I'm giving myself a pretty bad rap here. I would say about 90 percent of the time I'm a very calm and collected individual. But that remaining 10 percent of the time . . . where I'm not so calm and collected, those are the memories that will end up sticking out like a sore thumb to my impressionable children. They pick up on how I react to situations and that becomes how they will react to situations. They pick up on all my frustrations, anger, or irritations and it becomes theirs as well.

Remember, our children are observing everything we do and say at every moment of every day. It's not only what helps to shape their character but it's also a decider of how they will feel internally about themselves, about their worth. If we get angry and lose our cool over little insignificant instances such as these, we are inadvertently declaring to our children that the incident in question is more important than they are. Of course, it's totally not true . . . but that's what they'll think. That is how they will feel.

One day while I was folding a load of laundry, I suddenly heard a deafening crash echo throughout our house. Immediately after hearing the crashing sound, I heard little footsteps— pounding like the speed of light across our downstairs tile floor. I knew something disastrous had happened. I frantically ran down our staircase to see if my kids were safe and to find out where that deafening noise had come from.

My kids were supposed to be unloading the dishes from our dishwasher, but when I went down, all I could see was my daughter, Taylor, standing in the kitchen, staring at the floor, and my son, Trenton, over in our family room with his head smushed deep into the crevices of our couch. He was bawling so profusely that I was afraid he had been really injured somehow, as though a limb had been severed or something! I speedily ran over to my son and urged him to tell me if he was hurt in any way. Through Trenton's muffled wailing sobs, I could hear his tiny little voice whisper that he wasn't hurt. I needled him to explain to me what the loud crashing sound was. Finally, after what seemed like minutes of trying to pull himself together, he turned around and looked me straight in the eye, a look of terror and helplessness on his sullen face. He reluctantly explained to me that he had been trying to balance my favorite glass salad bowl on one of his tiny hands while simultaneously walking it to its designated cupboard to be put away. When, unexpectedly, it tipped off the palm of his hand and crashed to the floor, smashing it to pieces.

Now, again, at this moment, I had an instantaneous choice to make. I could immediately act on my anger and yell at him for being so irresponsible with my favorite bowl . . . like I really *felt* like doing. Or . . . I could take a moment, compose myself, and use this mistake in my son's judgement to teach him a life lesson that he could learn in no other way than to have experiences such as these. In that moment, I'm proud to say that I responded to this potentially hazardous situation in a manner which enabled both my son and I to have an invaluable teachable moment together and which left us both, afterwards, feeling happy and at peace. The Spirit was there guiding the conversation because I *allowed* Him to be.

Through this incident, I was able to teach Trenton about the Atonement of Jesus Christ, how we are all going to make mistakes in life. We'll all metaphorically smash some glass bowls during our lives here on earth. But that is why God sent His Son. For this precise reason! When we make mistakes, if we will turn to God and ask for forgiveness and seek His assistance, He will be there to pick up the pieces for us. Those broken bowls in our lives that look impossible to mend . . . they will be mended, and perfectly so. They will be made brand new again. That is the power of Christ's Atonement. He mends what's broken in us.

What a lesson to teach my little boy. There is no better teaching tool than experience. He felt the overwhelming grief of his mistake. He was inconsolable laying there on the couch, face down in shame . . . not unlike how he'll feel in the future over bigger and more spiritually damaging mistakes he'll inevitably make. But he knows now, through this tiny experience—and many others—where he can turn for repairs, where he can turn for peace. This lesson would not have been taught if I had let my rage and anger get the best of me as I did in the earlier example. This experience was well worth the loss of my favorite glass bowl.

Managing our emotions is a very difficult task and is a lifelong pursuit. It's especially difficult when sudden situations occur that we have not had sufficient enough time to process. We tend to react immediately, allowing the machine of our body to fly off the handle, while our rational mind takes the backseat. Our thoughts are the seed of all our actions, good or bad. If we learn how to meticulously manage our thoughts, managing our actions will be a piece of cake! This is why it's so important to walk away from situations where we feel a strong rush of negative emotions. We need a few moments (maybe longer) to get a grip on the situation so that our actions are a direct result of our carefully thought out brainwork and not a direct result of our adverse passions of the moment.

"Calmness of mind is one of the beautiful jewels of wisdom. It is the result of long and patient effort in self-control. Its presence is an indication of ripened experience, and of a more than ordinary knowledge of the laws and operations of thought."[1]

Charles W. Penrose wrote these inspiring words:

> School thy feelings, O my brother;
> Train thy warm, impulsive soul.
> Do not its emotions smother,
> But let wisdom's voice control.
> School thy feelings; there is power
> In the cool, collected mind.
> Passion shatters reason's tower,
> Makes the clearest vision blind.[2]

Our dear President Hinckley petitions us with these words, "I plead with you to control your tempers, to put a smile upon your faces, which will erase anger; speak out with words of love and peace, appreciation, and respect. If you will do this, your lives will be without regret. Your marriages and family relationships will be preserved. You will be much happier. You will do greater good. You will feel a sense of peace that will be wonderful."[3]

Our world is already filled with so much rudeness, anger, and hate. Let's not add to it with our unbridled passions and unruly tongues while we're in the moment. Instead, let's make it our goal to bring more happiness, love, and understanding into our families and into the world as a whole—for the only way to overcome darkness is by an influx of light. You and I can be the bearers of this light which will bless our lives and the lives of all those within our sphere of influence forever.

REFERENCES

1. James Allen, *As a Man Thinketh* (1903), 35.
2. "School Thy Feelings," *Hymns*, no. 336.
3. Gordon B. Hinckley, "Slow to Anger," *Ensign*, November 2007.

MOMS WHO LOVE DAD

"If you want something to last forever, you treat
it differently. You shield it and protect it. You
never abuse it. You don't expose it to the elements.
You don't make it common or ordinary. If it ever
becomes tarnished, you lovingly polish it until it
gleams like new. It becomes special because you
have made it so, and it grows more beautiful
and precious as time goes by."
—ELDER F. BURTON HOWARD[1]

I once heard Boyd K. Packer, while giving a talk on marriage, say, "I think of the girl who suffered a hectic and uncertain courtship, and on her wedding day she said in rapture and joy, 'Oh mother, at last I am at the end of all my troubles!' Wherein the mother replied: 'Yes my dear, you just don't know which end.'"[2]

Marriage is hard. No matter how great you think you are, no matter how awesome your man is . . . it's hard. I would say it's one of the hardest things we'll ever do. Marriage is taking two people who grew up completely different from each other—in families that most likely had very different rules, different ways of doing things, and different family dynamics—and putting them together. It's taking two people with two entirely different mindsets, two separate sets of experiences, and two different sets of strengths and weaknesses, then throwing these two people together in a metaphorical blender and basically saying: "Combine all these differences and work it out. Good luck!"

It's truly a humbling experience but . . . I think *purposefully* so!

The natural man (or woman) is all about self. It's the "What's best for me?" attitude. In order to have a successful marriage, this mindset needs to be ripped out of us, chopped in a million pieces, and thrown into a smoldering bonfire, never to be heard from again. We need to flip that whole philosophy on its head and learn to have the "What's best for *them*?" attitude. It's a difficult transition, definitely against your instincts, but it's one that needs to be made if we want to have not only a lasting marriage but, even more rare, a happy and joy-filled marriage.

Christ gave us the perfect example of how to act in our marriages. Christ was called the Bridegroom and we—the Church—His bride. What has He done for His bride? He gave His all—even His life—to save His bride. The ultimate "What's best for them" mindset (Ephesians 5:25–27). Marriage is one of the greatest training grounds for rooting out the "ME" mentality within us and truly learning how to gain the godly attributes of charity and self-sacrifice. Marriage is actually a blessing meant to transform our base characters into Christlike ones!

In the Church, we hold up eternal marriage and eternal families as the epitome of human attainment. The plan of salvation's end result is the eventual eternal glorification of the family. We get married in the temple for time *and all eternity,* but who would want to live for eternity in a miserable marriage? Not me! That reminds me more of the other place than of heaven! We need to make our marriages worth saving for all eternity . . . and the first step and the last step to doing this is to change ourselves. We can't change our spouse, as much as we may sometimes try. We can pray for them, yes, but we can't change them. Only they can do that with the help of the Savior. What is within our power though is for us to work on ourselves. Better ourselves. And hopefully, by seeing our concerted efforts, our husbands will desire to do the same.

"Men are that they might have joy" . . . right!? (2 Nephi 2:25). So what can we do to help this scripture be true of our marriages?

If I had to create a motto for marriage, I think this would have to be it: *Neglect Not or You Will Have Not!*

What happens to your house if you neglect it for even a week? Are you kidding me? It turns into a dump, a giant trash heap! Smells emanating from who knows where. Mice and cockroaches start to infest. It's nasty! What happens when you neglect your yard for even a short period of time? Noxious weeds start to take over the lawn and choke out any healthy plants that are growing there. *The same is with our marriage if we choose to neglect it!*

Richard L. Evans stated, "All things need watching, working at, caring for, and marriage is no exception. Marriage is not something to be indifferently treated or abused, or something that simply takes care of itself. *Nothing neglected will remain as it was or is, or will fail to deteriorate.* All things need attention, care and concern, and especially so in this most sensitive of all relationships of life."[3]

Greg's absolute favorite thing is when he comes home from a long and tiring day at work and I immediately stop what I'm doing and run over to him with a big smile on my face and give him a huge bear hug and maybe even a smooch. Greg doesn't yearn for this because he's some untamed beast that wants a little action. No way! He simply likes when I do this because it shows him that he's important to me and that I'm excited he's home. He loves little actions that show my attention is solely on him. A hug, a rub on the shoulders, even a flirtatious slap on the buns! Small gestures like this are very important to him, and for our marriage.

How do you think I know this? It's definitely not because I'm a mind reader or a pro at this marriage thing! It's actually through my many failings as a wife that I have learned how to show Greg that I love him. Through many a long talk between the two of us, I have learned what is important to Greg in our marriage. And vice versa.

John Bytheway stated, "Marriage isn't any big thing; *it's a lot of little things*. Acts of kindness every day create a happy marriage."[4]

Think of the things you used to do to attract your hubby and make him feel special *before you were married* and continue to do those things throughout the life of your marriage . . . *even* if you're tired or busy! It will help him to know that you are still attracted to him and that he's still *your man*.

A lot of times, after years of marriage, we get comfortable with each other and kind of fall into a rut of complacency. We stop trying so hard because, after the "I do's", we feel we've got them pretty much locked up as being ours. We take for granted the relationship and the promises we made. To have a healthy marriage we need to climb out of this dry and dusty rut of complacency and embed life-giving nutrients back into the soil of our marriage. This nutrient-packed soil will bring forth the fruits of love, happiness, laughter, and joy not only for your marriage but also for the whole family.

Truman Madsen speaks of another important factor in a healthy marriage when he said: "Humor is the oil that smooths the frictions of life . . . the kind of humor that laughs at one's self and that acknowledges one's foibles—and finds them funny instead of tragic."[5]

Have you ever done something that, looking back in hindsight, was probably not the smartest thing; but when your husband points it out to you, of course you think "How dare he!" and a fight ensues for the rest of the night? I'm sad to say that I may be talking from a little bit of experience. But I'm pretty sure I'm not the only one with such experiences.

Recently our family was driving home from Chick-fil-A and I happened to be in the driver's seat. As I was making a left-hand turn onto our street, I noticed a bunch of glass in the road, like someone had shattered large cases of bottles in the middle of the street. Instead of swerving and driving around the disaster, I literally plowed right through the sea of glass . . . not even giving it a second thought. Greg, looked at me in astonishment . . . and—sounding a *little* irritated— asked, "Why the heck did you not drive around the glass?!"

I know you're all in suspense, wondering how I reacted. Well, let's just say that I should have listened to my better judgement that day, but I didn't . . . at least for a bit. My logical mind was saying "Yeah, that was totally stupid of me! Why didn't I go around the glass?!" But my emotional mind, becoming defensive at the perceived attack, put up a shield and drew out a sword . . . ready for war.

Luckily my emotional mind didn't last too long. After throwing out a few haphazard excuses, meant to defend myself against his somewhat less than kind tone and his blatant dis of my amazing driving skills, I forced my mind to shift gears and to focus in on the reality of the situation. It was stupid of me and we all knew it . . . why fight the truth? "Only by pride cometh contention" (Proverbs 13:10). I knew it was my pride I was protecting, not the truth.

After this realization, I laughed and said, "You know what, Greg? You're right! That was pretty dumb of me!" And I proceeded to crack a joke about my old age and failing eyesight. We all laughed together at my comment, which was like pouring cool water on a growing fire. And we were able to have a great rest of the night together. My first inclination was starting to cause contention, but my second inclination eased it! Always strive to choose the road that will ease the building tension . . . no matter whose "fault" it is. Most likely it'll be a mixture of the both of you.

Madsen continues, "Instead of getting rigid and defensive . . . laugh at yourself. Acknowledge that you just made that foolish mistake. It's wholesome, it blows the pretenses away. It cleans out the carburetor in your life. You laugh with each other, laugh at yourself, acknowledge stupidities—they occur frequently at my house. Humor enables us to have proper perspective and to have vicissitudes and failures and get past them. But being rigid, sullen, and unyielding, that is the way to an early grave. Humor—cultivate it—restore it to your home if it's been lost."[6]

I think it's always important to keep in mind that we've married fallible human beings that are slowly trudging up the path of perfection one step at a time. Daily they will slip up, fall, and have to get back up and start climbing the rocky path again. We should try to be a little more compassionate and understanding of these weaknesses and frailties—even if they are offenses against us! Why? Because our husbands are in the same boat we are! They too, have married fallible human beings! We are on that same rock-strewn path and we too fall short of who we should be daily. We emotionally injure those we love on a regular basis because we are human and weak and tired and at times our nerves are wound so tight from stress that we snap. But just like Christ is forgiving, understanding, and patient with us—we need to be that way towards others—especially our spouses. Again, this is what contours our characters into becoming more like Christ.

Neal A. Maxwell once counseled the Saints to not look at the Church as a rest home for the already perfected. I think this is wise counsel for those in a marriage union as well. Marriage is a learning laboratory and a workshop in which we gain experience as we practice on each other in the ongoing process of perfecting ourselves.

We can further this metaphor by stating that the *marriage partners* are what constitute the "clinical material" that is essential for growth and development. We practice on each other and learn from each other and from our successes and our failures. Then we try to do better the next time after we have learned what does work and what doesn't work.[7]

Elder Bednar, working off of Elder Maxwell's quote, stated:

> Understanding that the [home] is a learning laboratory helps us to prepare for an inevitable reality. In some way and at some time, someone will do or say something that could be considered offensive. Such an event will surely happen to each and every one of us—and it certainly will occur more than once. Though people may not intend to injure or offend us, they nonetheless can be inconsiderate and tactless. You and I cannot control the intentions or behavior of other people. However, we do determine how we will act. Please remember that you and I are agents endowed with moral agency, and we can choose not to be offended.[8]

One of the most accurate quotes on marriage was stated by the English preacher/historian, Thomas Fuller. He remarked that it would be wise to "keep thy eyes wide open before marriage; and half shut afterward."[9] This semi-comical statement has a lot of truth to it. When you're in the dating stages of a relationship, it's important to discern whether or not your man has a good and faithful heart *before* you agree to tie the knot. Once you're married, if you already know that your husband *deep down* has a good heart, it's a lot easier to blow off or purposely overlook any minor weaknesses your spouse may have or offenses they might give off. You just chalk it up to being an imperfect human being just as you are. You then hope and pray they do the same towards your many blemishes and offenses.

Truman Madsen once stated, "If your marriage lacks and you feel like it has diminished, then do the things that will restore it and increase it. And if you say I don't love him anymore . . . then do the things that will cultivate that love."[10]

Joseph Addison remarked, "Two persons who have chosen each other out of all the rest, with the design to be each other's mutual comfort and entertainment, have, in that action, bound themselves to be good-humored, affable, discreet, forgiving, patient, and joyful, with respect to each other's frailties and perfection, to the end of their lives."[11]

These are just a few secrets I have learned along the way to have an overall happy and joy-filled marriage! Put these few simple tips into action and see how your marriage blossoms. It may take time, but if you really commit yourself to this goal, you will eventually reap the rewards of your dedicated sowing.

REFERENCES

1. F. Burton Howard, "Eternal Marriage," *Ensign*, May 2003.
2. Boyd K. Packer, "Eternal Marriage" (Brigham Young University devotional, April 1970), speeches.byu.edu.
3. Richard L. Evans, *Richard Evans' Quote Book* (Shepherdsville, KY: Publishers Press, 1971), 16; italics added.
4. John Bytheway, *What We Wish We'd Known When We Were Newlyweds*, (Salt Lake City, UT: Deseret Book, 2015); italics added.
5. Truman Madsen, *The Awesome Power of Married Love*, audiobook (Salt Lake City, UT: Deseret Book, 2005), CD, 2:00–6:30.
6. Ibid.
7. Neal A. Maxwell, "A Brother Offended," *Ensign*, May 1982.
8. David A. Bednar, "And Nothing Shall Offend Them," *Ensign*, November 2006.
9. Thomas Fuller, *Introductio ad prudentiam: Part II* (1727), 1817.
10. Truman Madsen, *The Awesome Power of Married Love*, audiobook (Salt Lake City, UT: Deseret Book, 2005), CD, 2:00–6:30.
11. Evans, *Richard Evans' Quote Book*, 16.

MOMS AND SONS

"Be a mother who is committed to loving her
children into standing on higher ground than
the environment surrounding them."
—MARJORIE PAY HINCKLEY[1]

On October 8, 2007, I received the best birthday present of my life . . . and I received it from God. I was given my amazing son, Trenton. He wasn't wrapped up in a box covered in "Happy Birthday" wrapping paper—with a bow placed neatly on top. Nor did I receive him in a gift bag with frilly tissue paper popping out the top. (That would be a little weird!) He was handed to me after months and months of excited, and a little anxious, anticipation. He was wrapped in a little swaddling blanket and placed on my chest. I remember just staring at his face in amazement and disbelief at how perfect he was. He wasn't perfect to me because of his perfect features: his beautiful eyes that stared up at me, his tiny fingers and toes, his perfectly shaped ears, his long shock of brown hair on top of his *slightly* cone-shaped head. No, he was perfect in my eyes because he was mine. I couldn't believe that this little heavenly angel was really mine! A true gift and responsibility from God.

The day of Trenton's birth had already been scheduled a month or so in advance. My doctor was going to be out of town during the period of Trenton's estimated due date and October 8—my birthday—happened to be the only day he would be working in the hospital close to his due date. So we decided that I would be induced. I was excited at the idea of sharing my birthday with this cute little guy of mine! The day of anticipation finally arrived and, overall, it went really well . . . just not *completely* as planned!

The tougher older generation of mothers are going to think I'm a real wimp . . . but I'll be honest—I was planning on having an epidural to help ease the pain of Trenton's delivery. That, at least, was the plan. As I was laying in the hospital bed, waiting for the induction meds to kick in, I began to change my mind. I was feeling good, not too much pain. I started to think that maybe I could really do it without the epidural. Time passed, hour after hour. Each time the nurse came in to offer the epidural, I would resist it, telling her that I was going to go as long as I possibly could without the meds. Hours passed and Trenton was still no closer to popping out. Finally, my doctor suggested he break my water to try and speed up the process a little. And OHHH did it work!

Within ten minutes, I went from a dilation of two to a dilation of 10. Needless to say, intense pain ravaged my body within those brutal ten minutes and the nurse said it was too late to give me the meds. I was literally writhing around on my bed, thinking my body was going to rip apart! Unfortunately, I hadn't put in the effort to learn any fancy breathing techniques, considering I thought I would have an epidural by now. Sweat was dripping down my face and body like I had just ran a marathon. Greg, seeing me in such pain and not knowing how to fix it, did the best he could to fan me with a pillow. This is pretty embarrassing to confess . . . but at one point, Greg's arms were so tired from fanning me so frantically that he finally had to put the pillow down for a moment and take a breather. I wasn't having *any* of that! Seeing that he was slacking on his duty while I felt like dying, I threatened that he better pick up the pillow and start fanning or else! When he innocently tried to explain that he just needed a moment's break—I literally kicked him in the stomach like I was a member of the women's Olympic soccer team, to get him going again! From that moment, Greg *knew* I meant business. With a shocked expression and a little bit of a smirk, he immediately picked the pillow back up and started fanning. Just a little side note: I really am a nice person, I promise, but somehow a monster invaded my body during those brutal minutes.

After the ten minutes of intense torture, I felt Trenton about to pop out. Of course, no nurses believed me because they said it was way too fast. But finally, when they saw that I started pushing him out on my own, they decided they would finally listen to me and check. To their great surprise (but not to mine) Trenton's head was already halfway out! The doctor ran in with just enough time to catch him. They cut the umbilical cord, cleaned him up, and handed him to me. I *immediately* fell in love. All the pain and suffering I felt just a few moments before faded far, far into my distant memory. I had my baby boy and he was everything to me at that moment.

How can anyone measure the love of a mother? How can anyone grasp the depth of emotion a mother has for her precious child? A mother's love is truly immeasurable. It is beyond our finite words can express. Joseph F. Smith stated, "The love of a true mother comes nearer being like the love of God than any other kind of love."[2] Similarly, Elder Holland expressed, "No love in mortality comes closer to approximating the pure love of Jesus Christ than the selfless love of a devoted mother has for her child."[3]

Christ, when trying to get us to understand the incalculable depth of love He has for us, compared His love to that of a mother's love. "*For can a woman forget her sucking child, that she should not have compassion on the son of her womb? Yea, they may forget, yet will I not forget thee . . .* Behold, I have graven thee upon the palms of my hands; thy walls are continually before me" (1 Nephi 21:15–16; italics added). Christ was teaching us that even the immeasurable love of a mother is but little compared to the unfathomable love He has for His family. Yes, as unlikely and impossible as it sounds that a good mother could ever forget her child . . . it is much more possible than Christ forgetting us. And He proves it to us by showing us the scar-covered palms of His hands. Reminding us of the infinite sacrifice He made for us. The price He paid to become our Savior.

As much as we love our precious sons, Christ loves them even more than we do. He wants them all—each and every one of them to return safely back home to Him. He has given mothers a sacred charge and responsibility to do all that is in our power to teach our sons—His sons—how to overcome the binding and debilitating snares that Satan has laid for their destruction. We cannot let this sly serpent bite them, infusing his toxic venom into their innocent souls until they are left dead to all things spiritual!

The Prophet Joseph Smith prophesied that sexual immorality would be the source of more temptations, more buffetings, and more difficulties for the elders of Israel than any other.[4] Similarly, President Joseph F. Smith stated that sexual impurity would be one of the three dangers that would threaten the Church within.[5]

If we do not see the complete fulfillment of these prophecies in the days that we are living in right now . . . we are either blind or living under a rock! Sexual immorality of every disgusting form is surrounding our boys from the time they step one tiny little toe outside the door until the moment they return back to the safety of the home. Sadly, they even find it sometimes within their own supposed "safe houses" as well! How can they escape it? Their schools are infested with it. Modern music is infested with it. Movies and television shows are infested with it. Their smartphones, iPads, laptops, desktops, tablets and magazines are infested with it. How do they even stand a chance?!

The world teaches our boys that to become "real men" they need to act like the grown man-babies that so often live on the screens of their devices. Partying all the time, no real responsibilities, just following their pleasures wherever they might lead, which will supposedly bring them happiness in life. The world also teaches them that the women they should find most attractive are the girls that are sprawled out on the magazine covers and the movie screens. I think one of our greatest duties as mothers is to teach our young boys what true manhood is by showing them good examples of strong men—whether they be living examples, examples throughout history, or examples contained in scripture. We also need to show our boys what true womanhood looks like through *our* examples. Sheri Dew once stated, "How will our young men . . . learn to value women of God if we don't show them the virtue of our virtues? If we don't show them what kind of women will help them find the greatest joy and fulfillment in their lives, who will?"[6] We will, of course! As mothers, we must!

I don't know of any cooler story that shows the power that faithful mothers have in the lives of their precious boys than the account of the 2,060 stripling Ammonite warriors in the Book of Mormon. Seriously, those moms are my heroes! Because of the diligence these mothers had in teaching their sons, when the time came to put those teachings to the test, their sons were prepared with the knowledge and strength needed to pass with flying colors. This group of young boys—teenagers, really—were surrounded on every side by a vicious enemy that did everything in their power to rip the young boys down and destroy them. Just like our boys are today. But because these mothers taught their young sons what true manhood is, and because of the great faith and love that these mothers had for their boys, the enemy could not pull them down . . . not one! The enemy had no power over these boys to destroy them.

What made these young boys so powerful that even while grown men all about them were falling to their deaths, being cut down by an enemy hell-bent on annihilating them, these young boys were miraculously immune to the death blows of their assailants? How could this be?

The scriptures say, "They had been taught by their mothers, that if they did not doubt, God would deliver them. And they rehearsed unto me the words of their mothers, saying: We do not doubt our mothers knew it" (Alma 56:47–48).

The boys' first line of defense was their *unflinching faith in God* that they learned from the teachings of their beloved mothers. It acted as a powerful armor in defense of these faithful boys.

What other powerful teachings did these devoted mothers instill deep into the hearts of their stripling sons that, literally, saved their lives? The scriptures read that the boys, "covenanted that they never would give up their liberty, but they would fight in all cases to protect . . . themselves from bondage" (Alma 53:17).

These mothers taught their sons the importance of covenant making and covenant keeping. In a world so obsessed with "do what feels good" and "live your passions," a righteous mother teaches, "do what you know is right—regardless if it feels good" and "live your covenants—despite your physical passions." Wow! What a concept nowadays! These boys were taught from day one that if they faithfully made and kept their sacred promises to God, He promised in return to protect them *at all times* from the enemy surrounding them.

Continuing on with the same scripture, we learn that these awesome mothers also taught their precious sons to never give up their liberty and to protect themselves from bondage *at all costs*! What a powerful message to our sons in this day in age. Our boys are constantly surrounded by things that would enslave them, that would *in reality* take away their liberty and put them in bondage. Pornography, pleasures of the flesh, drugs, alcohol, fame, and fortune—all these addictions are just a few of the countless traps set by Satan to ensnare the body, mind, and soul of the children of God. "And he became Satan, yea, even the devil, the father of all lies, to deceive and to blind men, and to lead them captive at his will, even as many as would not hearken unto my voice" (Moses 4:4). We need to teach our children that each of these addictions are snares set by Satan, who is the ultimate Counterfeiter. His goal is to pull off the ultimate switcheroo! He promises God's children that they will find pleasure and happiness in each of these things while all the while wrapping his heavy chains tightly around them, one link at a time, until they finally look down and see that they are trapped with seemingly no way to escape.

Another teaching of these great mothers is mentioned in the scriptures: "Yea, and they did obey and observe to perform every word of command with exactness; yea, and even according to their faith it was done unto them; and I did remember the words which they said unto me that their mothers had taught them" (Alma 57:21). So . . . what had their mothers taught them? These amazing mothers, again, from day one, taught their boys the true spiritual principle of obedience—and the magnificent blessings attached to it. The scriptures record, "There is a law, irrevocably decreed in heaven before the foundations of this world, upon which all blessings are predicated—And when we obtain any blessing from God, *it is by obedience* to that law upon which it is predicated" (D&C 130:20–21; italics added). Meaning when we are obedient to any commandment of God, a blessing will be attached to it. Ezra Taft Benson phrased it this way: "When obedience ceases to be an irritant and becomes our quest, in that moment God will endow us with power."[7] This is the secret that these righteous mothers taught to their sons! This is why they had such great power to overcome their foes! The stripling sons were taught "to perform every word of command with exactness; yea, and even according to their faith it was done unto them" (Alma 57:21). Obedience equals blessings, exact obedience equals greater blessings. Simple arithmetic!

It is important to note that although not one son of these angelic mothers was killed in any of the horrific battles, while thousands of grown men lay lifeless on the battlefield, "There was not one soul . . . among them who had not received many wounds" (Alma 57:25). No matter how obedient and righteous any of us try to be, we are never going to be perfect. We are going to sin and get tripped up by Satan at times. God absolutely knew this. That is the precise reason He sent His perfect Son to us. To break the chains of Satan that have us bound tight. It is imperative that we teach our sons the importance of Christ's mission! That He specifically came down *for them* because He knew they would fall short and need to call upon Him for assistance. That's life! That although we try to do our best . . . we will mess up at times. But we can be healed again, just like the stripling sons, if we will look to our Savior for help.

As latter-day mothers, the responsibility God has placed on us is considerable. It is a calling that at times seems too heavy to bear. But it is absolutely worth every single moment of difficulty. Mothers have been uniquely called and qualified to teach, nurture, and guide these precious spirits down the path that will bring them safely home to their Heavenly Father's outstretched arms. We have an amazing blueprint to follow of righteous mothers who have already succeeded in their missions as mothers and who now show us the way to achieve it. If we will teach our sons what attributes make up a *real* man and what kind of woman will bring them lasting happiness. If we will instill within our sons an unflinching faith in God through our teachings and example. If we will teach them the importance of covenant making and covenant keeping. If we will teach them to *never* give up their liberty to Satan, who seeks to enslave them. If we will teach them that both their physical and spiritual safety is determined by the degree to which they are obedient to the commandments of God. And, finally, if we will teach them that when they falter—because they inevitably will—they should run to Christ in all humility, who will be waiting with open arms to heal them. Somehow, if we can have these teachings penetrate the deepest recesses of their hearts, our most precious sons will be as the stripling warriors of old and *not one* of them will be lost to the fiery darts of the adversary. What an excellent promise we are given!

> Their preservation was astonishing to our whole army, yea, that they should be spared while there was a thousand of our brethren who were slain. And we do justly ascribe it to the miraculous power of God, because of their exceeding faith in that which they had been taught to believe—that there was a just God, and whosoever did not doubt, that they should be preserved by His marvelous power. Now this was the faith of these of whom I have spoken; they are young, and their minds are firm, and they do put their trust in God continually. (Alma 57:26; italics added)

REFERENCES

1. Marjorie Pay Hinckley in Jena Pincott, *Mom Candy: 1,000 Quotes of Inspiration for Mothers*, (New York: Random House, 2013), 90–91.
2. Joseph F. Smith, *Gospel Doctrine* (Salt Lake City, UT: Deseret Book Company, 1959), 315.
3. Jeffery R. Holland, "Behold Thy Mother," *Ensign*, November 2015.
4. Joseph Smith, as quoted in Ezra Taft Benson, "A Witness and a Warning," *Ensign*, November 1979, 74–75.
5. Joseph F. Smith, *Gospel Doctrine* (Salt Lake City, UT: Deseret Book Company, 1959), 312–313.
6. Sheri Dew, *No One Can Take Your Place* (Salt Lake City, UT: Deseret Book, 2004), 33.
7. Ezra Taft Benson, as quoted in Kim B. Clark, "Deep Obedience," (devotional at BYU–Idaho, Rexburg, ID, April 19, 2011).

MOMS AND DAUGHTERS

"How will our young women learn to live as women of God unless they see what women of God look like, meaning what we wear, watch, and read; how we fill our time and our minds; how we face temptation and uncertainty; where we find true joy; why modesty and femininity are hallmarks of righteous women?"

—SHERI DEW[1]

From the very beginning of our marriage, Greg and I absolutely knew, without a doubt, that we wanted to start having children right away. Most newlyweds leave room for a little bit of a honeymoon phase. But not us! Nope! Three months after Greg arrived home from his mission we were married in the Redlands California Temple; and within a month of getting hitched, I was pregnant with our sweet little daughter, Taylor. We believe wholeheartedly that we were inspired to start having children right away, God knowing that I would lose the ability to bear children just a few short years later. If we had even waited one year—*one!*—we wouldn't have our son, Trenton.

The day finally arrived when Taylor was going to leave her warm and comfortable home inside my bulging belly and join our little family in the outside world. Greg and I were beyond excited as we anxiously anticipated our future lives with this precious little spirit from heaven that would make our family of two become a family of three. While waiting for Taylor to make her grand entrance, I was enjoying the luxuries of hospital life: watching movies with Greg and some other family members, eating the fantastic Jell-O cubes that were being brought to me by my helpful nurses, and really, really enjoying the epidural that was pumping through my body and, quite literally, taking every single ounce of pain away. I was loving life!

A number of hours into my relaxing hospital stay, Taylor's heart monitor unexpectedly started blasting. I had no idea what the loud beeping noise meant but naturally, I started getting pretty worried! I grew even more anxious when our nurse came hustling into the room to inform us that Taylor's heart was having problems. She explained that her heart kept speeding up and then slowing way down in rapid succession. She said it was a sign that Taylor was under some sort of duress. The nurse told us that if she wasn't out soon, they would need to perform an emergency C-section to keep her safe.

Of course, I immediately started to panic like most moms in that situation would. My heart started racing at the thought of my poor baby girl being in danger. Inevitably, the more stressed I became, the more stressed Taylor became. As the nurses and doctor were making preparations for a possible C-section, Taylor finally decided that she had had enough of this nonsense and wanted out! I tried my hardest to help her out, but the anesthesiologist gave me *so* much medicine, that I couldn't feel anything—literally, not a thing! I couldn't tell whether I was pushing or not. Finally, after what seemed like forever of trying to push, out popped our bluish-purple bundle of joy.

The weirdest thing happened next! The doctor quickly threw Taylor up into the air with a twirling motion like she was a football with a perfect spiral and caught her safely back in his experienced arms. Greg and I just stood there, mouths gaped open at what we had just witnessed. Seeing our surprised expressions, the doctor hurriedly explained that Taylor had had the umbilical cord wrapped tightly around her neck and was being choked to death . . . hence the bluish-purple coloring. The fastest way to release the tension, I guess, was to throw her up and simultaneously un-twirl the cord from her neck. After cutting the umbilical cord and cleaning her up, the nurses handed me my little Taylor and I was in heaven.

It was soon brought to our attention by the nurses that Taylor had very high levels of bilirubin in her blood, causing her to have jaundice. Her skin went from purple when first born to deep yellow within a day. For Taylor's first few days of life, she lived in a phototherapy incubator. The incubator had special blue lights attached to it that shined down on her, helping to break down the bilirubin in the skin. Greg and I would go visit her constantly in the NICU. She looked so helpless lying there underneath those harsh glaring lights with only a diaper and padded goggles to protect her sensitive eyes. After a few days, Taylor's bilirubin levels improved enough for us to be able to return home. I still needed to wrap her in a fiberoptic blanket for a week to help improve her bilirubin count, but things were definitely looking up.

Throughout this whole ordeal, from Taylor's semi-stressful delivery to her time underneath the phototherapy lights, I couldn't help but sense just how fragile she was. And it really scared me. I questioned my abilities as a brand-new mother. I didn't know if I would be wise enough and capable enough to take care of her the way she deserved. It's not like an owner's manual popped out with her! All I could really rely on was prayer, my husband, and my natural instincts. That would have to be enough.

It's nearly twelve years later, and Taylor has grown up to be a remarkably healthy and strong eleven-year-old. I no longer worry from day to day about her physical fragility. No way! She's almost my same height and can waste me in pretty much everything we do together, from swimming and basketball to her talents with the piano and acoustic guitar. She is growing into an active and capable young woman.

The thing that scares me to death now is not her physical fragility, but her spiritual fragility. Not because I feel she's weak spiritually—on the contrary, she has a very strong spiritual nature about her—but because I know Satan wants her, just like he wants to capture and enslave all of God's precious girls. He knows that if he can get the world's future mothers right now, at this young age, he will most likely get their children, and their children's children—all throughout the forthcoming generations.

How does Satan most effectively get girls around her age? Well, quite easily actually. He blinds them to their true natures, their true potentials, and their infinite worth. He tries to make them believe what the world is selling as the definition of true womanhood: that their intrinsic worth is inseparably connected with their outside appearance. And if they aren't what the world deems as beautiful, they are of less worth than the girl that is. It's the caste system Satan cunningly puts in place for the downfall of the female gender.

If we are trying to teach our girls that it's not our image but who we are on the inside that defines our character, and yet we focus day in and day out on our own looks, what do you think they will believe more—our words or our actions? We cannot be fixated on our perfectly highlighted hair, our exquisitely manicured nails, our flawlessly applied makeup, our size 0 waistlines, our designer clothing, our fancy cars, our immaculate houses, and what we're going to fix the next time we enter our plastic surgeon's office. We can't be fixated on these things or our girls will be as well! They have it hard enough being surrounded by it at school, with their friends, and in all the media they partake of. We shouldn't add to the list of bad examples.

We can't be focused on celebrity gossip and culture, raunchy reality shows, the movie/TV/music award shows that showcase the idols of the world. Satan purposefully throws out, front and center, false images, false idols, for our impressionable young girls to worship—just as he has done from the beginning of time. His goal: to turn their gaze away from the one true source of lasting happiness and cement it on the "whited sepulchers" of the world "which indeed appear beautiful outward but are within full of dead men's bones" (Matthew 23:27). This has been the downfall of God's people since the ancient days. God would plead with His people, through His prophets, to look to Him, their one true God, to find happiness, fulfillment, and meaning in life. But the people would instead cast out God's prophets, kill them, and continue worshipping their golden, corruptible, man-made statues.

Is it any wonder that the prophet Nephi added the prophecies of Isaiah to his writings after he was shown in vision the last days before the coming of Christ? Nephi tells us that the words of Isaiah are of great worth to not only the people of his day, but more critically, to the people in the last days! Nephi warns us through Isaiah's teachings that worldliness will be one of the greatest problems that will infect the women of the church in the last days. He says:

> Moreover, the Lord saith: Because the daughters of Zion are haughty, and walk with stretched-forth necks and wanton eyes, walking and mincing as they go, and making a tinkling with their feet—
>
> Therefore the Lord will smite with a scab the crown of the head of the daughters of Zion, and the Lord will discover their secret parts.
>
> In that day the Lord will take away the bravery of their tinkling ornaments, and cauls, and round tires like the moon;
>
> The chains and the bracelets, and the mufflers;
>
> The bonnets, and the ornaments of the legs, and the headbands, and the tablets, and the ear-rings;
>
> The rings, and nose jewels;
>
> The changeable suits of apparel, and the mantels, and the wimples, and the crisping-pins;
>
> The glasses, and the fine linen, and hoods, and the veils.
>
> And it shall come to pass, instead of sweet smell there shall be stink; and instead of a girdle, a rent; and instead of well set hair, baldness; and instead of a stomacher, a girding of sackcloth; burning instead of beauty. (2 Nephi 13:16–24)

Now doesn't that sound pleasant?! Ugh . . . yeah right! I know I don't want to be one of those bald and scabby ladies, that's for sure!

The thing is, this passage of scripture isn't meaning that we can't wear jewelry, fix our hair nicely, or have changes of clothing to wear. That's kind of obvious. It's not the objects that are the problem but the attitude and the heart of the women wearing them. The women are haughty. They walk with stretched-forth necks as though they are better than everyone else. What are their "secret parts" that the Lord discovers within them? In my opinion, it's their blackened, filthy hearts. It's the heart that's fixated on the images of the world. "For where your treasure is, there will your heart be also" (Matthew 6:21).

I'm sure there's no one reading this book that has a blackened, tar-stained heart like the women this passage speaks of. But each of us, to one degree or another, has been infected with the toxic poison of worldliness which leaves a mark on our hearts. We each care about our image and how we look and are perceived by others. It's within our carnal natures to care about these things. We need to recognize the symptoms of worldliness in our lives and strive to root it out of us to the best of our ability with the help of the Lord.

Remember, our girls watch our every move. That's how they first learn what it means to be a woman: by watching us. They imitate *us*! What *we* do, what *we* say, what *we* watch, what *we* listen to, how *we* spend our precious time. They will observe which direction our gaze is focused and be greatly influenced by it.

I'm ashamed to admit it, but in my high school years, I didn't dress so modestly. I grew up being a total tomboy, thinking I was so cool wearing baggy shorts and my older brother's T-shirts. I know, I can't believe I'm telling you this either . . . how embarrassing! But I still remember the middle of my eighth-grade year, when my dad decided to have one of those "talks" with me, informing me that he thought that I should probably try to dress a little more "girly." Oh, did he ever regret having that conversation!

The next week at school, I tried it out. I always had a good number of friends at school but I was always the more shy and quiet one in the group, so I felt like people didn't pay as much attention to me. I was like the little mouse that tagged along with everyone. The day I came to school in my new "girly" clothes, things changed. It seemed like all of a sudden, my number of friends doubled . . . it was like magic! Surprisingly, it seemed like all my new friends happened to be boys for some reason. So of course, with these miraculous new friendships, I thought that I must be doing something right!

I went a little extreme in my clothing choices in high school. And for some reason during this time, some girls who were once my friends stopped liking me and all of my remaining school friends ended up being boys. It got to the point that I felt I *needed* to dress that way in order to keep my friendships. I could see a big difference in the attention I got from my boy friends when I wore a sweatshirt and jeans compared to when I wore something a little more revealing. It's almost like that was *why* they paid attention to me. Not a good feeling! It made me even more self-conscious and insecure about myself. Feeling like I only had many of my friends because of how I dressed was way bad for my psyche. I hated the feeling of it. All these things felt like weights on my back.

I justified how I dressed by telling myself that I was a good girl on the inside. I never broke the word of wisdom or the law of chastity so I was fine. I thought I could be holy on the inside but look worldly on the outside. Better yet, I told myself, I could be a better missionary because I could show the world that I could be a really good person and simultaneously not be one of those "weird-looking" Mormons. Yeah, that was my convoluted mindset during my high school years.

Of course, I look back now at my former self and think, "What an idiot!" Why did I care so much about impressing others? It just made me look stupid, and, at the same time, made me feel bad about myself. But at least I'm able to use my experiences and the knowledge I've gained from maturity to teach my daughter what *not* to do. I'm very open with her about my stupidities! I want my daughter to be free from the restraints of caring about how she's perceived in the eyes of the world. Free from the chains of measuring her worth by the standard the world sets. I know the world will pull her down, but I'm determined to do all in my power to push her back up.

It's important to teach our girls to respect themselves and to dress in a manner that shows it. I think sometimes the word "modesty" gets a bad rap, as though it's synonymous with the words "nerdy" and "homely." At least that's how I looked at it in my dumb years. We have to break the stereotype that's placed on modesty . . . because it's absolutely not true! You can totally dress "fashionably" and modest at the same time! We need to teach our girls that! When we buy our girls booty shorts and tank tops to wear, not only are we telling them that they should follow what the world deems as beautiful, but we are also creating a way tougher transition when it comes time for them to decide whether or not to enter the temple and make sacred covenants with God. I've had a couple friends in particular throughout the years who've expressed to me the difficulty they've had in choosing to go through the temple, for the specific reason that it would mean having to buy a whole new wardrobe and having to dress in a manner they weren't used to—that is to say, modestly. Do we really want to make it more difficult for our girls to choose to enter the House of the Lord? I know I don't!

Another super helpful thing we can do for our girls is to inspire them to find talents and hobbies that they can really excel at and feel confident in so that they won't feel that their best attribute is their looks. It gives their minds something to focus on and work towards other than their appearance. If a girl grows up thinking that the greatest thing about her is her beauty, how do you think she will feel about herself once her physical beauty starts to fade with age? Her confidence and self-worth will fade as she no longer receives the false adulation from others in the world. But . . . if this same girl is confident not only in her looks but also in other talents and hobbies she has adopted throughout the years, she'll still have many things that will bring her happiness and contentment within herself for the rest of her life.

My dad used to recite a poem to me entitled *As to Looks*, and he would use the funniest voice while saying it that always made me laugh. He would recite it like this:

> Some folk in looks take so much pride,
> They don't think much of what's inside;
> Well, as for me, I know my face
> Can never be made a thing of grace.
> And so I rather think I'll see
> How I can fix the inside of me;
> So folks will say, "[She] looks like sin,
> But ain't [she] beautiful within!"[2]

I always knew that my dad wasn't trying to secretly inform me that I was "ugly as sin." That would be a little rude and disturbing! I understood that what he was covertly trying to cram into my mind was the importance of making myself beautiful from the inside out. That this was the most important and longest lasting beauty of all. We need to continually teach this to our girls. Because the world teaches otherwise.

The most important thing we can give to our girls, more important than anything else, is an accurate knowledge of who they are and *whose* they are. An understanding of their true worth and their purpose here in life. That their great worth was already determined long ago and there is nothing they could ever do to change that fact.

My parents once held a family home evening, probably around my freshman year of high school, that I will never forget. They started off by asking us children this question: "What determines the worth or value of something?" Before any of us could answer, they brought out some visual aids. They brought out a bag of rice and one of my dad's precious gold krugerrand coins. Then they brought out a piece of black coal and what looked to be a large diamond.

My parents then asked: "Which in these pairs of items do you think would be considered most valuable?"

Of course, the kids all shouted out in synchronization that the gold coin and the diamond would be the most valuable. My parents asked us to explain our answer. One of the kids answered something to the effect of, "Because the coin and the diamond are rarer than the rice and the coal, they are therefore more expensive."

This answer was followed by my parents asking, "So what if a nationwide disaster occurred and a devastating famine ravaged our land. What two items would be of greatest value then?"

The kids thought about the question for a moment and then replied that, given those circumstances, the rice, which could literally save a life, and the coal, which would provide heat and a cooking source, would be most valuable.

My parents then inquired: "What do you think people would be willing to pay for this bag of rice or the brick of coal in this scenario? Do you think they would be willing to barter this gold coin or this diamond for some rice or coal?"

We all agreed together that people would be willing to trade just about anything to survive during those harsh circumstances. Circling around to the first question they had asked, my parents questioned, "So, what then determines the worth of something?"

The kids finally came to the conclusion that the worth of an item is determined by the amount someone is willing to pay for that item. People are willing to pay more for precious gold coins and diamonds in times of plenty, but in times of hardship, people would be willing to pay much more for the food and heat source.

My parents then asked us, "What then determines the worth of an individual? *What determines your worth?*"

We all sat there in a stupor for a moment, then someone replied, "Well, I guess the amount someone is willing to pay for us, I guess?"

The true purpose of the lesson was then disclosed. My wise parents asked us if we knew what was paid for us. They then explained that God thought us of such great worth that He was willing to pay the *infinite price*. He paid for us with the life of His Son. That means that each one of us is of infinite worth. No matter our looks, no matter our talents, no matter our weaknesses, God paid the ultimate price for each individual, and our worth is invaluable to him.

If our girls knew this—I mean really knew this, deep down in the depths of their souls—*nothing* the world threw at them would be able to shake their belief in themselves or their testimonies of the gospel. Satan would never be able to grasp their hearts with his awful chains and pull them away from the truth of who they are and who they can become. They would be as a house that's built upon a rock, that when the rains, floods, and whirlwinds of life come to destroy, because their house is built on a firm foundation, the foundation of Christ, they would never fall. The storms would rage right past them and do no lasting damage. They would be a mighty force in the world for good.

REFERENCES

1. Sheri Dew, *No One Can Take Your Place* (Salt Lake City, UT: Deseret Book, 2004), 33.
2. John Kendrick Bangs, "As to Looks."

MOMS WITH "LOST SHEEP"

*"To those brokenhearted parents who have been
righteous, diligent, and prayerful in the teaching of
their disobedient children, we say to you, the
Good Shepherd is watching over them."*
—JAMES E. FAUST[1]

*B*LAST . . . ZOOM . . . KABOOM!
And everything came crashing down. Crashing down into burnt
dismal heaps of ruin.

A thing of beauty, a thing of wonder, a thing of magnificence . . .
now turned to ashes.

Fatal choices were made, and disaster was the inevitable consequence. Choices that would eventually be the cause of utter grief,
heartache, and complete misery for all parties involved.

What a sad narrative. What a disheartening tale. Only it's not a
tale—it's a real-life story. One that was told by President Uchtdorf a
few years back in General Conference, where he spoke of his experience as a little boy living in Germany during World War II.

He recounted the utter devastation which took place as thousands
of tons of explosives were dropped by Allied forces on the German
city of Dresden, a city not far from where President Uchtdorf grew up.
Dresden was given the nickname "The Jewel Box of Saxony" for its
stunning artisanship and magnificent architecture that had been built
up by wealthy kings over a thousand years. But now the "Jewel Box"

lay in heaps of burning rubble and ash, with over ninety percent of the city completely destroyed by the controversial aerial bombings which killed an estimated 25,000 German citizens.

President Uchtdorf said of this, "During my childhood I could not imagine how the destruction of a war our own people had started could ever be overcome. The world around us appeared totally hopeless and without any future."[2]

Hopeless. Without future.

Words that many a mother has felt in regard to her wandering, seemingly lost children. Children who were once innocent and pure—now captured by the cruel world that seeks their demise.

This sad story of the devastating loss and ruin of the once beautiful city of Dresden could be the story that countless mothers have been witness to as they see their precious sweet children make choices that they know will lead them off the path of happiness and ultimately down the path of sorrow, the path of ruin. Just as the city of Dresden was built stone after stone, each precious layer laboriously chiseled and lovingly placed through countless years of toil and effort—so too is the life of a mother.

Mothers spend day after day, night after night, year after year molding, shaping, building, and carefully contouring these precious jewels of theirs amidst constant blood, sweat, and tears. This they do happily, joyfully, and without any thought of monetary compensation because, to them, seeing the growth, development, and beauty that comes as the result of their constant efforts is their compensation. And it is worth more than all the accolades, luxuries, or wealth the world has to offer. A mother works tirelessly, but not for payment. No. A mother gives of her whole self, asking nothing in return. And she does it out of sheer love. The purest form of love. Love for her child that can only be matched by the love God has for each of us. A mother's love truly is Christlike love in every way.

What more does a mother desire for each of her children than a life of happiness and love? From even before the first tiny flutter she feels within her belly, that mother is daydreaming about who this little soul, clothed in mortal flesh, is going to become. This good mother would give her all, her everything—*even life itself*—if it meant that her beautiful child, her precious jewel, would be able to experience a meaningful, happy life, full of goodness, virtue, and accomplishment.

I cannot think of a more devastating reality for a mother than to have that child, the child of her heart, turn away from all that she lovingly taught. To turn away from all that is good and wholesome in the world. To see this child stumble, fall, and nigh unto the brink of spiritual death is almost enough to make this mother desire the grave for herself, rather than have to watch the full-scale descent of one she loves so much. There could be nothing more painful, more heart-wrenching for a mother, than to see her precious baby tread down forbidden paths that will take them further and further away from the one true path of freedom and happiness. Restricted paths that will ensnare the body as well as the soul and bind it to a life of darkness and servitude. A path that will inevitably take them away from the family.

> I have a family here on earth.
> They are so good to me.
> I want to share my life with them through all eternity.
> Families can be together forever
> Through Heavenly Father's plan.
> I always want to be with my own family,
> And the Lord has shown me how I can.
> The Lord has shown me how I can.[3]

These are the lyrics to one of the most sacred and beloved LDS hymns. It states our ultimate goal as Mormons. To live in the celestial kingdom with our Heavenly Parents, our eldest brother Jesus Christ, and our entire family someday . . . for all eternity. One big happy family! What could be better? What could be more desired than these holy aspirations? Nothing that I can think of, that's for sure! The gospel of Jesus Christ is completely centered around eternal families. Whole families being made clean through the atoning blood of our Savior and then living *together forever* with God. That's our highest aim as Latter-day Saints, which will bring us a completeness of joy in the world to come.

But what if we have children who choose not to qualify for a celestial life? Who seem to choose—at least for the moment—a different destination for their life's end than the one we have desired for them all our lives. They deny this gift from God. How can a mother's joy ever be complete with the loss of even one of her cherished children? Is there any hope? Is all feeling of being whole lost forever for this mother?

President Uchtdorf declares that all is NOT lost forever! There is always hope! And he tells us how: "Last year I had the opportunity to return to Dresden. Seventy years after the war, it is, once again, a "Jewel Box" of a city. The ruins have been cleared, and the city is restored and even improved."[4]

He told of visiting the beautiful Lutheran church, Frauenkirche, the church of Our Lady, which was originally built in the 1700s. This church had been one of Dresden's shining jewels, but the Allied bombings had left it nothing but a pile of blackened rubble. Sadly, it remained that way for many years until finally it was decided by the German people to restore this jewel back to its former glory. They rebuilt the church using the old ashy stones of the past, intermingled with the new beautiful stonework of that day.

President Uchtdorf describes, "Today you can see these fire-blackened stones pockmarking the outer walls. These "scars" are not only a reminder of the war history of this building but also a monument to hope—a magnificent symbol of man's ability to create new life from ashes."[5]

As he sat pondering the history of Dresden, its war-torn past that left it destitute of beauty and life, he was amazed at the resolve and determination of those who restored what had been so utterly and completely annihilated. At that moment, he felt the Spirit teaching him a deeper and more powerful lesson than that seen from the surface. He stated, "Surely, I thought, if man can take the ruins, rubble, and remains of a broken city and rebuild an awe-inspiring structure that rises toward the heavens, how much more capable is our Almighty Father to restore His children who have fallen, struggled, or become lost?"[6]

President Uchtdorf explained that it doesn't matter how completely ruined a life may appear from the outside; it doesn't matter how deep the wounds of sin may have penetrated; no matter how lonely, how desperate, how broken, or without hope and without God a life may seem—this life can be made whole and clean again.[7]

A life can be reconstructed and made even more beautiful, even more stunning than it had been formerly. It can be rebuilt by the greatest of all architects: the Architect who first designed and carefully planned out the magnificent structure that is this human being. The Architect who first saw the innate potential of this soul before it was even born on this fallen earth.

What joyous words for a mother to hear! God can rebuild anyone who allows Him to pick up the broom and start sweeping away the ash. Anyone who will allow Christ to gather up the crumbled bricks of their life and start refashioning them into a beautifully ornate structure again.

The religious leaders of Christ's day continuously rebuked the Savior for spending time with people who they labeled as sinners. In the eyes of the judgmental Pharisees and scribes it may have seemed as though Christ was perhaps accepting or even sanctioning their irreligious behavior. Uchtdorf analyzed that maybe these leaders had some sort of distorted belief that by condemning, ridiculing, and shaming these sinners, it would somehow help them down the path of repentance.[8] Perceiving their thoughts, the Savior told this parable:

> What man of you, having an hundred sheep, if he lose one of them, doth not leave the ninety and nine in the wilderness, and go after that which is lost, until he find it?
> And when he hath found it, he layeth it on his shoulders, rejoicing. (Luke 15:4-5)

What was it Jesus was trying to teach the people, both Pharisee and sinner alike, as they gathered around the Savior to listen to His words?

"Is it possible that Jesus's purpose, first and foremost, was to teach about the work of the Good Shepherd," President Uchtdorf questions? "Is it possible that He was testifying of God's love for His wayward children? Is it possible that the Savior's message was that God is fully aware of those who are lost—and that He will find them, that He will reach out to them, and that He will rescue them?"[9]

If so, what must the wandering sheep do to deserve or qualify for the help of the Good Shepherd? President Uchtdorf answers:

> The sheep is worthy of divine rescue simply because it is loved by the Good Shepherd. To me, the parable of the lost sheep is one of the most hopeful passages in all of scripture. Our Savior, the

Good Shepherd, knows and loves us. He knows and loves you. He knows when you are lost, and He knows where you are. He knows your grief. Your silent pleadings. Your fears. Your tears. It matters not how you became lost—whether because of your own poor choices or because of circumstances beyond your control. What matters is that you are His child. And He loves you. He loves His children.[10]

You may feel as though your children are lost, maybe even lost forever . . . but it's not true.

Christ, the Good Shepherd, knows exactly where they are, He knows their circumstances, and knows their heart.

If there is even an unseen flicker of light left within them, He can illuminate that flicker until it's as intense and magnificent as the blazing sun.

He knows how to soften their heart like no one else does, and He's working on it. But only He who has eyes to see within the deepest chambers of the human heart can recognize the tiny seeds that are being embedded and the watering that's covertly taking place.

Only He knows the time of the harvest within their souls. Only He knows when the fruit will be fully ripe and ready to be picked. Whether it's in this life or the life to come, it will happen. Repentance will need to take place . . . godly sorrow felt . . . but it will happen. And it will happen when the time is right *for them*—not for you. As hard as that is to hear for a mother.

Jeffery R. Holland stated, "However many chances you think [they] have missed, however many mistakes you feel [they] have made . . . I testify that [they] have not traveled beyond the reach of divine love. It is not possible for [them] to sink lower than the infinite light of Christ's Atonement shines."[11]

So . . . what can we as moms do in the meantime, while the Good Shepherd is working on the heart of our child? Two words: *love them!* We need to love them for who they are, not for who we wish they would be. No strings attached.

Gordon B. Hinckley once stated, "Love is the only force that can erase the differences between people or bridge the chasms of bitterness."[12]

What else can we do? Two more words: accept them! We need to accept them despite their faults . . . just as Christ accepts us despite our faults. I love these words by Edwin Markham:

> He drew a circle that shut me out—
> Heretic, rebel, a thing to flout.
> But Love and I had the wit to win:
> We drew a circle that took him in![13]

Even if it feels as though your rebellious child is pushing you away through the choices they're making, open your arms up wide and gather that disobedient child deep into your circle of love and acceptance. Help them *know* and *feel* that you love and accept them for who they are . . . without conditions.

Is there anything else we can do? Three words this time: *see the good!* A close friend wrote these words:

> When our youngest daughter came to live with us for three months last summer, I was a bit concerned that it might be a difficult adjustment for her . . . and for us! She had lived on her own for several years. She ate only vegan. She had blue hair. She had tattoos. She had a tiny nose ring. She wore clothing not [up to] our church standard. And had friends foreign to our church standard of thinking.
>
> At first, communication was stilted, untrusted a bit. But shortly the barriers melted with each other's honest empathy. Discussions, acceptance, growth, understanding. Both her father and I learned to adore her as our child of light, with her own free agency, creativity, and adventurous spirit. She introduced us to new adventurous things we would never before have tried ourselves.
>
> We worked to focus our attention on her heart, rather than on the choices she made that were contrary to our beliefs. We opened up our eyes and we were able to see her in a new light.
>
> She has a giant capacity for love of all. Every person, no matter what ethnicity, gender, station in life. But she especially has a love for those she sees that are in need. She prefers the underdog. She is a pit bull to those who menace and prey on the innocent.
>
> After graduating college, she got a job working at a homeless shelter. She would write grants, give speeches in multiple communities in hopes of receiving grant money for their homeless shelter.

She and some of the other employees at the homeless shelter would walk around the city sidewalks in the middle of extreme snowy winters to register each homeless person in their city. They made sure each knew about the services, including sleeping facilities, offered at the different homeless shelters in their communities. These 'walk-a-bouts' had to start at 5:00 a.m. so they could catch people 'on the spot' before they would leave for the day.

She received special training and taught high school students the importance of rejecting bullying, recognizing sexual predators, and teaching what to do to be a proactive, protective, participant in alerting authorities safely if they witness sexual abuse. She taught how not to be a silent bystander.

She worked next with abused women and children's outreach. She helped protect and enable them in all ways needed as provided by her organization and the government.

My husband and I could feel a paradigm shift coming on. My mind physically, mentally, and spiritually felt and recognized it. We had to be humble, non-judgmental, and realize that we were being taught sweet lessons by the Spirit. Lessons on how to see our daughter the way our Savior sees her. Looking for the good in her heart rather than focusing on her bright blue hair, tattoos, and piercings.

We realized that she *walked in the footsteps of the Savior but did not recognize whose light had guided her there.*

My life views slowly expanded like a sunrise on the distant horizon. It was the love of Christ growing in our hearts for our daughter that finally was able to crack open the hardened feelings that had been accumulating without us even knowing. We had a new enlarged vision of how the Savior views our daughter. And it is with love. Always love. And hope. Hope that through these life experiences she will come to recognize at some future date whose light it is that has been guiding her footsteps toward the downtrodden of the earth. Whose light it is who inspires her to walk with outstretched hands, reaching down into the dark abyss to pull up individual after individual into the light of their self-worth. I believe that she will come to know these things someday. And I will love her and have faith in her until that glorious day of recognition finally comes.[14]

My dad, as a little boy, lived in Heidelberg, West Germany, shortly after World War II. My grandfather, who had served his mission in Germany years before, worked for the Department of Defense and was sent to Germany as diplomat, helping to rebuild the fallen government in that land. He had absolutely loved the German people and their culture ever since his mission and was heartbroken over their collapsed state. The German economy was in shambles. German citizens destitute, with little food to feed their families. My grandparents, from time to time, would hear a knocking at their back door. When they would open, it would be a German citizen seeking to barter a precious family heirloom for some food rations. Because of this, my dad's family left Germany with a number of beautiful German relics.

Among the antiques my grandfather acquired from his time in Germany was a precious porcelain teapot. It was made from Dresden porcelain, which is known to be one of the top of the line grades of porcelain. Dresden porcelain is, of course, made in Dresden, Germany— where Elder Uchtdorf's remarkable story took place.

At first glance of the Dresden teapot, you are in complete awe of the graceful shape, the intense blue and gold coloring, and the intricate details that went into the creation of this beautiful masterpiece. Even at second and third glance you are amazed at this piece of German craftsmanship. But as you slowly turn the antiquated teapot around on to its other side, you begin to notice blackened ashy scars running up the sides of half of the timeworn teapot. Scars left, my grandfather was told, from the Dresden incendiary bombings during the war. This teapot was a precious jewel that had been extracted from the "Jewel Box" after the flames of the fires had died, and the city was left in ruin.

That little teapot was damaged. Yes. It most certainly was. It had been burned and left scarred from its earlier life. And yet, when I look at it—or when anyone else in my family looks upon it—it is beautiful, priceless, of infinite value. And this, made even more so because of its scars, not in spite of them. *Because* of its history, notwithstanding it! We can physically see where it came from just by looking at its scars, but we can also see how far it's come to where it is now. We can view the path that led it from the prejudice and hate of war, back into the warm hands of safety, security, and love of a family.

Is this little teapot worth more or worth less from its hard knocks in life? To me, this little teapot has a greater story to tell than it would have otherwise, without the scars of its past.

So it is with each of us. Each and every one of us has scarring. Scarring from earlier experiences that left us injured and in need of the Physician. These scars are left as monuments to how the children of God can overcome, move forward, and progress on the road towards our ultimate destination of becoming like our Heavenly Parents and eldest brother, Jesus Christ.

Even our Savior, after he was crucified, ministered unto his Apostles by first showing them the scars on his hands and feet and the wound at his side. This He did so they would recognize that it was truly Him. "And when he had so said, he shewed unto them his hands and his side. Then were the disciples glad, when they saw the Lord" (John 20:20).

These scars, left as a monument for all to see. To see His past and know what He had done for them, so they could have a future. Simply because He loves them, the obedient and the wanderer alike. Because in truth, we are all lost sheep in need of our Shepherd's guiding hand to lead us back into the arms of safety and security with our loving Heavenly Family.

There is a beautiful picture that hangs in the Provo Temple. This picture is of the Savior and the woman taken in adultery. The woman kneels low to the ground as she is being mocked and shamed by the judgmental and hypocritical Pharisees. The Savior lovingly stands over this woman, His gentle hand extended towards her, waiting patiently for her to grasp it. He sees that this is one who is in great need of His love, and He offers it freely. If you stand close to the painting, you can see a tear falling from the left eye of her upturned face.

Christ is not excusing her past actions. No. But He is having compassion for her fallen state. My definition of true charity is being able to put myself in someone else's shoes. Feeling their shame, feeling their embarrassment, feeling their sorrow, and treating them as I would want to be treated if the roles were reversed. That is what our Savior does in His perfect charity. He doesn't ignore sin, but He is able to have compassion for it. He is able to look beyond the frailties and weaknesses of a person, have pure love for that individual, see their potential, and treat them as the holy being they can be. He says to them, *Go, and be better. Be that child of light I know you truly are. I have taken your sins from you and you can now walk a higher path.*

What hope this can bring to the wearied heart of a mother. Christ stands above each of us in our fallen state with his hands lowered, awaiting the day when we will take hold so that he can lift us out of the ruin and sin of our past lives. To rebuild us, heal us, and make us new again. To turn our ashes into a beautifully ornate "Jewel Box" again.

Mothers, please don't beat yourselves up thinking you have somehow failed as a mother because you have a child that has wandered off. You are in good company with some of the best parents around. The prophet Lehi and his wife Sariah had children that wandered. King Mosiah had children that wandered. Alma the Elder had a child that wandered. There are no perfect parents that I know of, except two: Our Heavenly Parents, and they had one third of their children wander off and choose another path. So please, stop blaming yourself. Have hope. Have faith. Have love . . . and all will turn out well in the end.

The lyrics of this song by Natalie Grant speaks the heart of every mother on this mortal sphere who has experienced the heartache as well as the longing for hope for a wayward child.

> You can rise up from the ashes
> Make something beautiful
> Of all the broken pieces
> And I'm believing you'll come running
> Into the arms of Jesus
> You were made to shine
> You were made for life
> Even if you've lost your way
> Turn and you will hear love say
> You were made for more
> So much more
> Child of everlasting light
> Made to blaze away the night
> So baby, burn bright
> Burn bright
> I'm believing you'll come running
> Into the arms of Jesus.[10]

REFERENCES

1. James E. Faust, "Dear Are The Sheep That Have Wandered," *Ensign*, May 2003.
2. Dieter F. Uchtdorf, "He Will Place You On His Shoulders And Carry You Home," *Ensign*, May 2016.
3. "Families Can Be Together Forever," *Hymns*, no. 300.
4. Dieter F. Uchtdorf, "He Will Place You On His Shoulders And Carry You Home," *Ensign*, May 2016.
5. Ibid.
6. Ibid.
7. Ibid.
8. Ibid.
9. Ibid.
10. Ibid
11. Jeffery R. Holland, "Laborers In The Vineyard," *Ensign*, May 2012.
12. Gordon B Hinckley, *Standing for Something: 10 Neglected Virtues That Will Heal Our Hearts and Homes* (New York: Times Books, 2000), 3.
13. Edwin Markham in Gordon B. Hinckley, *Standing for Something: 10 Neglected Virtues That Will Heal Our Hearts and Homes* (New York: Times Books, 2000), 8–9.
14. Anonymous personal acquaintance, in discussion with the author, October 2017.
15. Natalie Grant, "Burn Bright," recorded October 2013, track 5 on *Hurricane*, Curb, compact disc.

Family
is not defined
by our genes...

it is
built
through
love

MOMS WHO STEP UP

*"Biology is the least of what
makes someone a mother."*
—OPRAH WINFREY[1]

Abraham Lincoln once stated, "All that I am or hope to be, I owe to my angel mother."[2] Could any mother ever hope to have a more beautiful sentiment said about them from one of their children then those words spoken by Lincoln about his mother?

Any true history connoisseur will be able to tell you who exactly the quote above is referring to. The quote does *not* refer to Lincoln's biological mother but instead it refers to his stepmother, Sarah. Abraham Lincoln's birth mother died when little Abe was just nine years old, leaving him motherless until his father, Thomas, remarried a short time later to Sarah Bush Johnson.

Sarah was able to fill the enormous void in Lincoln's life after the loss of his biological mother. Sarah loved young Abe and inspired him to cultivate the God-given intellect and talents she saw hiding within him.

Author Jeff Oppenheimer said of Sarah, "She recognized a boy of tremendous talent and saw the diamond when virtually everyone else around this gangly, awkward boy saw the rough. . . . That's what mothers do." Lincoln later confided to a relative that his stepmother, "had been his best friend in this world and that no son could love a mother more than he loved her."[3]

What a testament to the tremendous power a stepmom can have in the lives of the children she *voluntarily* gathers into her heart.

All mothers are expected to give their full love and devotion to those little ones that have been borne to them. It's as easy as breathing to give your love to someone who's an extension of yourself. Who you carried within you, feeling all the kicks and flips, hiccups and hunger pangs, for over nine months. What's more natural?

A good stepmom is a special breed of woman. She opens her whole heart to children that carry another woman's DNA. She gives her mind, body, and soul to children that, many times, don't recognize or appreciate the efforts and see you as a second-class citizen compared to the mother they came from. It's anything but natural.

Some moms are asked to step up after the untimely death of a beloved mother, as Sarah Lincoln was. But let's face it, a large majority of mothers are asked to step up as the result of an untimely death of a marriage. In my close circle, I am truly blessed to know an angel mother who stepped up to the plate when another mother stepped out.

As a child growing up in the Church, you have all these expectations cultivated in your mind of how your life is going to look when you grow up—whether you're male or female. Temple marriage, a whole herd of children being born to you, and happily ever after—throughout time and all eternity. But guess what? Life has a funny way of not always turning out exactly how you'd hoped or planned. That's life—and there's really nothing funny about it at all!

I've seen one of my very closest friends go through this exact situation.

Justin did everything seemingly right in the eyes of our Mormon culture. He served a mission, met a girl while he attended institute, and got married in the temple. They had four tiny children right away and then . . . *SMACK*! She left to make a new life for herself.

My friend was utterly and completely devastated, with four tiny children who now looked to him—and him alone—to not only be the provider but also the mother figure in the home. He reluctantly moved back into his parents' house, humiliated and ashamed to show his face around town and *especially* to show his face in the home ward in which he grew up.

I can imagine the thoughts that must have been going through his mind. *What will they think of me? What will they be saying behind my back? They'll think I'm a complete failure as a husband and father!*

Justin felt like dying. Just fading away into existence so he didn't have deal with the reality of his new situation. But he couldn't. He had his four young boys to think about. They had just been left too, and by the one person who was supposed to love them the most in all the world. My friend knew he needed to put on a strong front for them.

Justin still remembers his first Sunday back at church. He walked in with his parents, his four boys tagging along behind them. He was trying to keep his face down, maintaining a low profile so that maybe, just maybe, nobody would notice him walk in. After sacrament meeting was over, he quickly walked out of the chapel, making his way down the hall toward his next class. When to his surprise, someone quickly grabbed his arm and pulled him off to one side of the church building.

It was a brother in his ward that his family had known for years and years. This brother spoke one simple sentence—just one. But to Justin, it was as though he had just been delivered life-sustaining water as he lay there helpless, near death, in the dry and arid desert of depression.

This man wrapped his loving arms around my friend and simply stated, "Justin, you're a hero to us all." He then walked off, leaving my friend with tears running down his flushed cheeks.

This simple sentence gave my friend the strength to go on when he didn't feel he could.

Humans are interesting creatures. When things are going well in life, we tend to forget our reliance on the Lord. I've noticed, especially within my own life, that it's the struggles, the hardships, and pain that help knit my heart with God's. Those are the times that I turn to God the most, seek that relationship with Him, when I have nowhere else to turn. It's sad but true. Justin was no exception. I had never seen my friend so full of hope, so full of faith, and so reliant on the guidance of the Spirit, as I saw him during those most difficult and trying of circumstances.

He pled with the Lord *continually* to help him know how to make this right. He begged the Lord to bring a mother into the life of his boys—not for his own sake, but for theirs. They desperately needed the influence of a good and faithful mother in their lives. A mother who loved them no matter their faults. A mother who cared more about the needs of those little ones than the desires she had for herself.

Justin cried unto his Maker for a miracle.

And the Lord answered by sending them Anna. Beautiful, angelic Anna.

I know Anna will laugh or maybe even cringe when she hears me calling her angelic, but it's true. At least that's the way those closest to Justin feel about her rescue of him and his four boys. She sacrificed her life of complete freedom to save those who were in a desperate situation and could not find their way out of it.

Anna was this beautiful 35-year-old woman. She dated many guys throughout her young life but had never found the one she felt she was to marry. She was this carefree girl who was used to hanging out with her unmarried friends until all hours of the night. Driving down to the beach all the time for bonfires, going to the movies, eating lunch out every day in between appointments at work. Life was seemingly good.

In the midst of all this freedom, all this fun, she knew that something was missing from her life. She desired to know her purpose. She wanted to find her mission in life.

When Anna met Justin and his four boys, she finally felt like she had found her calling: to love Justin with all her heart and to be the mother these boys needed in their lives.

Despite warnings from friends and family about the difficulties she would face joining a blended family, she prayed unto the Lord for guidance and she felt like she received her answer.

It wasn't easy for Anna to transition from being an independent, single woman, to all of a sudden being thrown into not only the role of wife, but simultaneously taking on the role of full-time mother to four boys ages three, five, eight, and ten. No grace period. No time to get used to married life. Nope! It was, "Here is your wedding ring" one day, and, "Here is your mini-van for taxi duty" the next. Of course it would take some getting used to . . . *a lot* of getting used to!

When telling me her story, Anna said this:

> It was really difficult to adjust from being able to do whatever I wanted, whenever I wanted, to being thrown into the confines of dropping off and picking up from school. Plus all their homework . . . that was a real adjustment! Watching over them every night was also a big change in lifestyle.
>
> I struggled with the whole concept of what's mine is yours . . . and, to be honest, sometimes still do! If I put something in a drawer and then go back to get it a short time later, chances are, it's probably no longer in that drawer. All of the neatly organized office supplies would be used and thrown to the wind for whatever school project, craft/art project, or destructive project they've come up with that day. They would go through my stuff when I was out and take whatever they found interesting. That was definitely a change to what I was used to!
>
> Meal planning is essential when you're on a tight budget and it's tricky to cook for kids.
>
> Anna explains that before she was married, she was used to eating out a lot, whether with friends or just by herself. And when she did eat at home, preparing a meal would be a cinch—because she would only be cooking for one. It was a huge change to go from cooking for just herself, to now cooking for a whole herd of picky boys!
>
> When you have kids from birth you get to know what their tastes are and they are used to the kinds of foods you cook. When you come in to the middle of it, you have to just go for it and hope they like something. I feel like I'm a pretty decent cook so when they would complain...I would get really frustrated! I always served them their food and gave them a little bit of whatever I made and expected them to eat all of it. I felt like this prevented all of the extra snacking that kids tend to do right before bed.[4]

Anna saw that her desire to make them eat all the food she served them was causing a lot more contention than she was hoping for. She continued:

> I still make them eat whatever I've prepared, but they get to dish up their plates now and choose how much they are going to eat.
>
> It also helps that I've now had time to figure out a lot of what they like. It takes time. One kid however, will probably never like

anything I cook. He chokes down 90% of what I make and tries to hide his disgust. I won't lie . . . it's a little maddening! I have a theory that kids' taste buds are formed at a young age and they tend to stick with that palate. Every time the kids visit their mom, I get to hear about all of the amazing food she made for them. It's really super annoying but I just put on my happy face and smile through gritted teeth.[5]

Many stepmoms have a difficult time knowing how to deal with the biological mom. Every family has different dynamics. In some families, both moms get along really well to the point that they're good friends. This, of course, is the ideal situation. Other times, one or both of the moms may be a little sneaky and manipulative because they feel threatened by the other mom. Ideal situation? Yeah . . . not so much! Most moms, I would venture to guess, are somewhere in between the two of these extremes. Anna has learned a few tips along the way that she says work well for her family when dealing with the bio-mom.

The first rule is to "NEVER speak badly of the bio-mom to the kids." Anna states, "If you can't say something nice, don't say anything at all. A mom is an extension of you. If someone says something bad about your mom, they are saying something bad about you. You're not hurting *her* when you say negative things—you are really hurting the child."[6]

On top of hurting the child, you're also hurting yourself. Does it really make you feel any better about yourself when you pull her down? Of course not . . . so don't do it! You should want to be a happy and positive person in the lives of your family, not a drain. It only makes you look bad when you speak badly of the bio-mom, not them.

The second rule that she advises is to have Dad always be the one to handle Bio-Mom. "If travel arrangements need to be made, kids need to be dropped off, Dad should always be the one to do it. Arrange it at a time when he is available to do it and not when it means the step-mom has to step in and do it."[7]

Anna's third rule is for those who co-parent. She says, "Bio-Dad and Bio-Mom have to hammer it out. Step-mom can give her opinion to Bio-Dad but she should never get involved beyond that. If you are entering into the step-mom role and you know that both biological parents are heavily involved in parenting their kids, you just uphold the rules as best as you can."[8] This will help to keep the peace between both parties.

Discipline is another tough subject to address for many step-moms. Anna describes:

> I realized along the way that I had to make my husband be the one who disciplined the kids. With him at work all of the time, this makes it really difficult. We have had to come up with pre-emptive strikes. He would come in with consequences ahead of time and emphasize emphatically that I was in charge and whatever I said was the rule. We have had these same discussions over and over… and still do. We've learned that the kids need to be disciplined from their parent every time. Even if there was an incident that the step-parent took care of earlier in the day, the biological parent needs to readdress the issue with the child to drive it home.[9]

What about when children are born into the new family? That can sometimes add another layer of difficulty to the family dynamics. Anna describes:

> When I had a child of my own, there was a definite shift in the house. I could not control the bond I felt with my own biological child. She was all mine from the start! There were no adjustments with her because I was her only mom. The bond is instantaneous. It was so easy that way. Having felt and experienced that, it was now a matter of learning how to create that same bond with the other kids. One interesting thing I have learned is that having a biological child has taught me how to truly love a child. So knowing how to love her has taught me what to do in certain situations. I can tell myself that I wouldn't be upset at her for doing this or for doing that…so I shouldn't get upset at them for doing it. Also, if I would be really happy with her for doing this thing or that thing, then I should show my excitement for them accomplishing it as well. I always try and apply this formula to the situation at hand.[10]

Some stepmoms may question whether God will assist them in mothering their stepchildren as much as He will assist mothers who are raising their own biological children. Anna explains:

I feel like Heavenly Father wanted me to be the mother of these children. So there have been many times when I felt like I knew what was best for them in a way that only a mother knows. I can sense when they are up to no good and I can sense when they are having a hard time with something. I can feel the Spirit guiding me in ways that are going to be the most helpful to the children. This is something I pray for regularly. I am always asking Heavenly Father to help me know how to help them and know how to fulfill their needs.[11]

There are times it can be difficult to notice the blessings you're receiving from taking on this role of mother to those that weren't born to you. When you're deep in the trenches and the war is still going on with the bullets and bombs flying overhead. Sometimes the children don't make it easy for the stepmom to join the family because of their obvious allegiance to their birth mother. But remember to not take it personal. Most of the time it's not *you* that they don't like, it's the *situation* that they don't like. The children most likely are hurting inside from the breakup of their parents and you are a reminder that their parents will never be getting back together. That is hard for kids to process and accept. There is adjustment that needs to take place. Anna has said that although she is in the middle of the battle right now, she has seen "glimpses" that help her to push on when times seem tough, such as the following experience:

We have had a terrible time with our oldest child. As soon as he started seminary, however, we noticed some changes. He was reading his scriptures regularly and he was beginning to soften. After he went to EFY the change was more than obvious. We were sitting in sacrament meeting and I looked over and found him reading his scriptures. I knew then that his testimony was solidified. He started to behave in a kinder and more relaxed manner. He gave a talk in church that he wrote all by himself. I can't remember what he said but I cried with joy and pride through the whole thing.

It was that one moment when I said "This is why I do what I do. This is worth the fight." My ultimate goal is to make each of my children responsible adults with strong testimonies of the gospel and of our Savior. If I can do that, I will have succeeded. That is where I will count my blessings because I will have achieved what I believe the Lord wanted me to do.[12]

You may feel like you've been dropped in shark-infested waters and you're struggling to stay afloat. You may feel like you're not appreciated and not accepted by the children you have opened your heart and life to. You may wonder if you're actually making a difference in their lives.

It may look as though they aren't listening to you. But they are. It may look as though they don't care about you. But they will.

If they see you take a real genuine interest in who they are, their hobbies, their interests, the things that get them excited in life—they will eventually learn to trust you. If you do all you can to look past their faults and to see the beautiful child of God they are on the inside . . . they will be able to feel this from you. Throughout the years, they will grow to respect and admire you because you first showed them the respect and admiration you desired to have. Your prayers for them and your example to them will stick with them all their lives. And you will truly be a force for good throughout their lives.

Abraham Lincoln again said of his loving stepmother, Sarah, "I remember my mother's prayers and they have always followed me. They have clung to me all my life."[13] That's the power of a dedicated stepmom. You can see their influence in the lives of the children who were raised by these wonderful moms who chose to step up.

REFERENCES

1. Oprah Winfrey, https://www.brainyquote.com/quotes/quotes/o/oprah winfr106855.html.
2. Abraham Lincoln in Josiah G. Holland, *The Life of Abraham Lincoln* (1866), 23.
3. Jeff Oppenheimer in Christopher Klein, "The Two Mothers Who Molded Lincoln," last modified May 9, 2014, http://www.history.com/news/the -two-mothers-who-molded-lincoln.
4. Anna Doe, in discussion with the author, October 2017.
5. Ibid.
6. Ibid.
7. Ibid.
8. Ibid.
9. Ibid.
10. Ibid.

11. Ibid.
12. Ibid.
13. Abraham Lincoln in Richard L. Evans, *Richard Evans' Quote Book* (Salt Lake City, UT: Publishers Press, 1971), 12.

MOMS WHO DISCIPLINE

"If you teach a child how to govern his own behaviors, you will teach him how to change his heart. This change of heart is more important than any behavior change."
—NICHOLEEN PECK[1]

A short time ago my family was invited to attend our friend's evangelical church for their little girl's baby dedication. We were so excited to be a part of this special day for them. After the dedication, their pastor, Pastor Justin Frailey of City Church, stood up and dropped some major truth bombs that I wish *every* parent throughout the world could hear and learn from. It would revolutionize parenting in a huge way!

It was family month at our friend's church, meaning that for the whole month, each sermon would be focused specifically on issues that dealt with family life. The Sunday my family attended, the whole sermon was focused directly on the critical nature of disciplining our children. I found it seriously ironic because *literally* the next day, I was going to start writing this chapter on discipline. The timing was pretty miraculous!

The pastor started off by talking about sports. Most sports, if not all sports, have boundaries or lines you CANNOT cross or you'll be considered out of bounds. No matter how amazing a catch is, a kick is, or a swing is, if the ball goes out of bounds the game is momentarily stopped, the ball called back, and the point discounted. Staying within bounds is absolutely critical to the rules of the game.[2]

Staying within bounds is also crucial to the game of life. Life is chock-full of boundaries. There are moral boundaries that are vital to follow, such as being honest in all your dealings with your fellow men; financial boundaries that are crucial to live by, like never spending more money than you bring in; marital boundaries that are imperative to any healthy and long-lasting relationship, such as staying true and faithful to your spouse; and the list goes on and on. There are specific boundaries we need to stay within if we desire to have successful, productive, and happy lives. Crossing any of these boundaries will sooner or later bring the consequences of disappointment, regret, and misery to one's life and to all the lives affected by those choices.

Pastor Frailey stated that "self-discipline is the ability to live in-bounds in an out-of-bounds world."[3]

Or in other words, self-discipline is the ability to govern one's own actions in a world that celebrates crossing the lines.

King Solomon, who is looked to as one of the wisest men to ever walk the face of the earth, spoke these astonishing words: "Whoever spares the rod hates his son, but he who loves him disciplines him diligently" (Proverbs 13:24 ESV).

What?! If you don't discipline your son you hate him? That sounds a tad harsh! Why would Solomon say such a thing? Well, it turns out that he saw firsthand the ramifications that await those who have a total lack of discipline in their adolescent years. Three of them happened to be his brothers Amnon, Absalom, and Adonijah—each of whom lost their lives due to the fact that they had not received the invaluable gift of self-discipline from their parents.

Their father, King David, continuously closed his eyes to the unruly behavior of his children. In fact, in 2 Samuel, David finds out that his son, Amnon, raped his daughter Tamar, and this was his reaction: "When David heard what had happened to Tamar, he was very angry. But Amnon was his oldest son and also his favorite, and David would not do anything to make Amnon unhappy" (2 Samuel 13:21 CEV).

Really?

He raped your daughter but you don't want to make him sad in any way, so you stay silent?! C'mon, David!

Amnon obviously lived his early life not feeling the restraint of boundaries, so he thought that he could just take whatever he wanted without the fear of consequence. He ended up paying for his father's lack of guidance with his life when his brother, Absalom, found out and killed him for it.

Another instance was when David's son, Adonijah, planned a coup to take over his brother Solomon's appointed throne. One might wonder how Adonijah would have such gumption to take it upon himself to seize the throne from his brother. 1 Kings 1:6 reads, "His father had never at any time displeased him by asking, 'Why have you done thus and so?'" David never once questioned Adonijah's choices. Never once throughout all his adolescent years did he think it wise to ask his son, "Why did you make that horrible decision?" And again, this lack of parental guidance ended up costing Adonijah his life.

Pastor Frailey explained, "Solomon is reminding us that the purpose of parenting and discipline is to ultimately raise self-disciplined adults. In fact, we're not raising children, we're raising adults! They are children for a short amount of time and then they are going to be launched out into the world and you hope that you have loved and disciplined them enough that they are able to function as a self-disciplined adult."[4]

I think when we're children, and in the midst of regularly being disciplined by our parents, we don't quite grasp the "It's for your own good" concept. No matter how many times our parents repeat that phrase to us, following the doling out of a well-deserved punishment, we just don't see how the penalty we earn could possibly be for our own good! In my adolescent years, I looked at disciplinary actions more as my parents' way to get me back for not obeying them than anything else. Probably for this reason, my parents one night decided to hold a family home evening that was solely based off one scripture in Hebrews.

The scripture read: "For whom the Lord loveth he chasteneth, and scourgeth every son whom he receiveth" (Hebrews 12:6–8 KJV).

After this scripture was read, I remember being somewhat shocked and a little confused by it. I had never heard it before. I didn't understand why our loving Heavenly Father would choose to chasten and scourge those whom He supposedly loved. Those words sounded harsh and mean to me. They seemed like the polar opposites of the word love in my immature mind. As we discussed the meaning of the scripture as a family, the scope of my youthful understanding began to deepen just a bit, and at least on a surface level . . . I began to grasp the concept of *Parental Discipline=Parental Love*.

Now, as an adult, and having children of my own, I fully grasp this concept—because I have an understanding of the purpose of parenting. If a teacher never corrected a child's homework, how would that child ever grow and become better? If a teacher never informed the child which of his answers were incorrect, how would the child ever know which problems he needed to study up on and fix before the next test? He would go into the test thinking all was well. Thinking that he knew exactly what he was doing, and exit in complete shock after finding out his dismal results. He wouldn't have a clue what he had done wrong to receive such a grade. This wouldn't be fair to this poor student, and it's not fair if we, in like manner, do this to our kids. We will handicap them for life if we don't teach them acceptable behavior and lovingly correct them when they fall short of it.

Our pastor friend spoke of four different ways parents tend to discipline their children.

The first is the *"Low Affection/Low Discipline"* group, or what Pastor Frailey calls a "Zombie Parent." These parents are not engaged in their kids' lives at all. They don't put forth effort to love their kids and they don't put forth effort to correct their kids. They are just kind of there, doing their own thing and allowing their kids to do their own thing. You find a plethora of the people who fill our nation's prison cells had parents like this—completely absent in just about every way.[5]

The second group is the *"Low Affection/High Discipline"* parent. This is the hardcore authoritarian parent. This parent sets clear boundaries and structure, but rules over their child like a dictator rules over his subjects. This parent is stern most of the time and holds back their affection. Children in this situation usually end up resenting the parent's authority and eventually rebel against them as they grow in age. It's not a healthy situation to be in. They "reprove with sharpness" but never "show forth afterwards an increase of love toward him whom [they have] reproved."[6]

The third is the *"High Affection/Low Discipline"* parent. This parent loves on their kids a ton but doesn't love them enough to correct them. They never set clear boundaries or consequences for their children to live by. These kids grow up knowing they're loved, knowing that their parents think they're amazing, and thinking that they deserve to have anything they desire just for being them. They believe they can do whatever they want, whenever they want—no consequences attached—because they're *special*. These kids grow up to be adult-children. They have a fun childhood but as soon as they enter the adult world, they soon find out that they're just as special as everyone else, and the outside world won't baby them like their mommy did. It will be like a kick in the gut when they learn that their college professors and boss won't bow down to their every whim like they're used to.[7]

The fourth group is the *"High Affection/High Discipline"* parent. These parents know that "Discipline isn't something you do *to* your child, it's something you do *for* your child." These parents show great affection towards their children. But they love their kids so much that they put forth the extra effort of setting boundaries and consequences for their children to live by . . . *and they stick to them!* These kids will grow up knowing that they are loved by their parents, but they will also grow up knowing that there are consequences attached to every choice they make, whether good or bad. They will know exactly where the boundaries lay, and they will learn through trial and error why it's in their best interest not to cross over the boundary line. When they grow up and leave the house, they will actually be adults who know how to govern their own actions. This will be a priceless gift received by the child, given by those who love him dearly.[8]

Pastor Frailey expounded:

> You better find some boundaries that you can put in [your children's] lives and you better put some teeth to it where they understand that 'this is the line and I can't cross it.' It is absolutely necessary that you develop boundaries where they know you mean

what you say—and you say what you mean…because by doing this, we are actually loving our children. If you don't discipline them, somebody else will. When they turn 18, it might be a penitentiary, it might be a gang, it might be a mean employer, but somebody else is going to bring down the hammer and do what you should have done when they were in your life. And when they get disciplined by somebody else, that other person is not going to hug him afterward and reconcile with him and let them know that they're loved, because the world is harsh and cruel. Adonijah got spanked, but it wasn't by a loving father that actually loved him. He was executed for his rebellion. Because a life without boundaries ends in ruin.[9]

Again, he explained, "The goal of parenting is not to get my kids under my thumb but it's to raise up my kids to become successful adults that actually win in life. . . . It's to equip them with healthy boundaries . . . and to help them understand the power and value of boundaries."[10]

If we're hoping to raise disciplined children, it's critical that we become disciplined ourselves, because "undisciplined parents breed undisciplined children."[11]

Pastor Frailey informs us of three different kinds of undisciplined parents. Each of us have fallen into these traps at one time or another throughout our parenting journey.

His first group is the *"Lifeguard Parent."* This parent is always trying to step in and rescue their child from the consequences of their bad or neglectful actions. An example of this is a parent that will drive to their child's school to drop off homework that was thoughtlessly forgotten at home by the child. Yes, this may be an embarrassing moment for your child when they have no homework to turn in. Yes, this may lower their grade in the class. But in the long run, what will your *not* rescuing do for them? It will make them realize that mommy won't save them when they are careless and it is *guaranteed* to make them put more thought into remembering their homework the next time.[12]

The second group is the *"Etch-A-Sketch Parent."* These parents, just like the toy they're named after, draw lines and then erase the lines. The boundaries are always in motion. Being here one minute, then being removed and replaced over on the other side the next moment. Could you imagine if the boundaries of a football field kept moving?! Players would never know whether they were in bounds or not. Kids will never know what is or is not acceptable if the parent never creates a firm boundary. This creates confusion in the home and frustration in both child and parent. We need to firmly set the law, inform our children of our expectations and the consequences affixed to the breaking of the law, and above all else, we need to be *consistent*! The Bible says that a double-minded man is unstable in all his ways (James 1:8). We need to not be double-minded. Our minds need to be fixed on our end goal of helping our children learn to self-discipline.[13]

The third group is the *"Split-Decision Parent."* These parents are many times not unified in their disciplining methods and their kids know it and use it to their advantage. They try to play each parent like a fiddle, one against the other, to get what they want. One parent is usually left looking like the mean authoritarian and the other parent is usually seen as the sympathetic hero that tried to save the day for the child. This can create major friction within the home and resentment between the parents—especially from the parent that always feels like they have to be the bad guy. Parents need to *work together* to set boundaries and the consequences that are attached to them and then both parents need to stick to them. If an issue comes up that was unforeseen, parents need to discuss the situation together and agree upon a solution—*out of earshot of their children.* That way, they come to their child as a united front, neither parent looking better or worse to the child. This child will know, without a doubt, that both parents mean business and it would be fruitless to pit one against the other.[14]

All children have different personalities, so a consequence that works for one child may not work for another child. Similarly, family dynamics are different from family to family. A consequence system that works for one family may not work for another family. All I can speak from is my own individual experience.

My family has used a consequence system from the very beginning of our children's lives that has worked like a charm, at least for us. One of the most important parts of our system is the setting of boundaries.

Greg and I are very adamant in *continually* explaining to our children what are acceptable forms of behavior and what are not. As we're driving on our way to church, we talk about it. On our way driving to their learning center, we discuss it. Our kids know the lines that we have set and they know what our expectations are.

Secondly, we have clear-cut consequences that are attached any time a boundary line is crossed. My kids know that they have no warnings when it comes to choices that break actual commandments, such as if they choose to be dishonest. And my children know that they have one warning when it comes to smaller crimes such as being rowdy at church or forgetting to do something they were asked to do earlier.

If they continue on after that warning, then *snap*! Their treats are gone the rest of the day. When I say treats, I mean anything that my kids value the most. For my kids, it's any sugary-sweet treat as well as their ability to play, listen to, or watch anything on an electronic device. They know this and accept it . . . although they are not thrilled about it. If they continue on with this behavior even after losing their treats, next comes the loss of their snacks. This means they eat nothing besides breakfast, lunch, and dinner for the rest of the day, or if it's later in the day, they lose their treats for the following day. If for some very strange reason the bad behavior *still* continues after the loss of their treats and snacks (which it very rarely ever does) then they are sent to their room until they have a change in attitude.

After the conclusion of their fixed consequence, we make sure to always sit down with them and discuss the situation. We make sure that they know that it was not we who gave them the punishment, but instead it was they who *chose* this consequence for themselves because of *their choice* to break the rule. You want your kids to understand that you are not the bad guy here. You are simply enforcing the consequence that they previously agreed upon. All of this should be done with a calm and loving voice so they don't "esteem thee to be his enemy." So they know that "thy faithfulness is stronger than the cords of death" (D&C 121:43–44). They need to know you love them all throughout the disciplining process and you need to be fully committed and consistent to this process, or else all your half-hearted efforts will be for naught.

Our true goal in disciplining our children is to work on the heart of our children. We want our children to eventually learn to *desire* to stay within bounds rather than just being fearful of the consequences they'll receive from crossing the line. We want them to have no more disposition to do evil but to desire to do good continually, because it is who've they've finally become, after years and years of making mistakes, fixing mistakes, and starting all over again afresh.

Nicholeen Peck stated, "If parenting is about punishments, then parenting is only a battle for control. Our real responsibility as parents is to communicate a reason for a change of heart in our children."[15]

Hebrews 12:11 reads: "Now no chastening for the present seemeth to be joyous, but grievous: nevertheless afterward it yieldeth the peaceable fruit of righteousness unto them which are exercised thereby."

We have been given authority for a very short time to manage God's children here on this earth. Our role as parents is to direct and guide our children on to the path that will lead them back home to their true Father, their Heavenly Father. Through faithfully disciplining our children with love and tenderness, our children will eventually reap the rewards of true and lasting discipleship.

REFERENCES

1. Nicholeen Peck, *A House United: Changing Children's Hearts and Behaviors by Teaching Self Government,* (Seattle, WA: CreateSpace, 2009), 3.
2. Pastor Justin Frailey, "Sermon on Discipline" (presentation, City Church, Riverside, CA, September 24, 2017, https://www.facebook.com /CityChurchRiverside/videos/10156080704202985/).
3. Ibid.
4. Ibid.
5. Ibid.
6. Ibid.
7. Ibid.
8. Ibid.
9. Ibid.
10. Ibid.
11. Ibid.
12. Ibid.
13. Ibid.

14. Ibid.

15. Nicholeen Peck, *A House United: Changing Children's Hearts and Behaviors by Teaching Self Government*, (Seattle, WA: CreateSpace, 2009), 3.

MOMS WHO BUILD CHARACTER

"Society's problems arise, almost without exception,
out of the homes of the people. If there is to be a
reformation, if there is to be a change,
if there is to be a return to old and sacred
values, it must begin in the home."
—GORDON B. HINCKLEY[1]

We have a famine consuming our nation. Not a famine of food or of water, but a famine that is even more poisonous, even more deadly than the lack of physical sustenance. This famine is infesting and killing off all that we hold dear in this world. Our country, our people are starving from an extreme lack of moral character. We can see the deficiency within our government, our businesses, our entertainment, our schools, and sadly, within many of the homes in our nation. These influential institutions are seemingly on life support, dying of moral malnutrition. Both our overflowing prison cells and the plentitude of litigation suits are just two of the many ramifications of this moral drought.

Gordon B. Hinckley asked, "Can there be any doubt that a great sickness has invaded our land, and that healing is desperately needed in our hearts and in our homes? Our value system is deteriorating and crumbling before our eyes."[2]

Character was once taught to children in their homes, as the family sat around the smoldering light of their wood-burning stove, reading the Bible together and actually—believe it or not—conversing together as a family. Now, families are so busy with work, sports, school, friends, TVs, computers, video games, smartphones, and other extracurricular activities that it's a triumph if they even hang out in the same room for a few minutes together, let alone sit down and have a group discussion on character building. Families prioritize their busy lives, and the premeditated teaching of character building is pushed way to the bottom of the list. Families are just too busy for that sort of thing.

This lack of moral character can also be blamed on the "Great Decline"[3] of religiosity within the United States. People just don't go to church like they used to, nor do they hold to the tenants of the Bible as they once did. The Bible used to be the number one reading text for children in school. Most children actually learned how to read by using the Bible as their main curriculum. First, listening to the Bible being read to them as young children and then learning to pick out words from amongst its pages as they grew in age. Kids knew and memorized the teachings contained in the Bible just as kids nowadays know and memorize the words to the latest Taylor Swift single. Kids within our nation's public school systems are no longer allowed to read anything that has to do with promoting religious values in school, especially if it's Christianity. Public schools are totally secularized.

President Hinckley explained, "For a good while, there has been going on in this nation a process that I have termed the secularization of America. The single most substantial factor in the degeneration of the values and morals of our society is that we as a nation are forsaking the Almighty, and I fear that He will begin to forsake us."[4]

My children's homeschool charter program gives state educational funds to the families who are a part of their program. We use these funds to purchase any curriculum we desire for our children, as long as it does not mention anything about "Christian values." Anything that alludes to teachings in the Bible is *strictly forbidden* and cannot be purchased with these educational funds. Heaven forbid we teach our children any biblical values mixed in with their math, science, grammar, and history.

Margaret Thatcher, former Prime Minister of Great Britain, said on multiple occasions, "You use the name of Deity in the Declaration of Independence and in the Constitution of the United States, and yet you cannot use it in the schoolroom."[5] She definitely recognized our hypocrisy and called us out on it!

Moral values are now extracurricular, I guess. Something you can choose to teach on the side, if you feel like it. Morals should, in no way, be combined with the essentials such as language arts or physical education in a classroom setting, right? What baloney! I don't know about you, but if I had to choose, I would much rather my child learn moral integrity than any other subject they could possibly learn throughout the day, because morality is what decides who my child is as a human being . . . not just what he or she will do to earn a living later on in life. Of course, learning both secular knowledge and morality are both indispensable in the life a child. But if I had to choose, I would much rather have a son or daughter who lacked an abundance of wealth but was morally strong, than a child who became wealthy through their secular knowledge but lacked moral fortitude.

Morality is the foundation whereon a life is built. If the foundation is solid, then no matter what happens to us in life, the ups and the downs, we will be able to stand strong and have the confidence to look ourselves in the mirror at the end of each day without feeling ashamed. If the foundation is faulty, if we have lied, cheated, and been dishonorable in our dealings with our fellow men in order to get gain, then no matter how successful we become in the eyes of the fickle world, our lives will threaten to break apart at any moment and with every gust of wind that comes our way. Not only will we not be able to look at our own image in the mirror without feeling a sense of shame, but we will not be able to look at the faces of our loved ones without our consciences being seared from a sense of overwhelming guilt.

It's our responsibility as mothers to build strong character within our children from the earliest of ages. It's not the duty of our kids' school nor is it the duty of their Sunday School teacher. It's ours! If we will instill these traits within them from the very beginning, then it'll become a part of who they are as people when they grow to adulthood. It's much more difficult to do a patch up job later on, when our children are less malleable, than to form them correctly from the start. If we want to heal our nation, we need to begin by placing our emphasis back on our children's moral education. We need to emphasize values such as honesty, strong work ethic, charity, humility, perseverance, self-control, and respect. These are just a small sampling of the countless virtues that are taught within the pages of scripture.

A person who has these values ingrained within their character knows that the main purpose of gaining their secular education is to then go forth and serve humanity with the knowledge and expertise they have gained. On the other hand, a person who has not developed these lofty virtues within themselves inevitably gains their secular knowledge only to serve themselves, to gratify their worldly and carnal ambitions. Secular knowledge without moral integrity is a dangerous thing. And sadly, our highest institutions are filled with people that fit that description.

So what can we as mothers possibly do, not only to teach our children these honorable virtues, but to make those virtues live and grow within the hearts and minds of our tender children? I had two excellent examples while growing up—my mom and dad— who taught me, in their own individual ways, what it means to have character and the importance of it in our lives.

My mom was constantly filling our house with music, pictures, books, and other materials that would help us children feel the spirit on a daily basis. Any direction you turned within my house you would find a picture, a statue, or a quote of something uplifting to the soul. Beautiful, Spirit-filled music would always be heard emanating throughout our house, whether from the CDs she bought to use in the family player or from the dozens upon dozens of gospel-centered CDs she bought for us to play as we got ready for seminary in the early morning hours of the day. Our refrigerator was literally covered with scriptures and quotes that—whether we liked it or not—we were forced to see, if we ever wanted to grab a bite to eat.

One quote, in particular, that she placed on our fridge always stood out to me whenever I would take the time to read it while scrounging around for some food. The quote was from the first president of Brigham Young University, Karl G. Maeser. The quote read: "I have been asked what I mean by 'word of honor.' I will tell you. Place me behind prison walls—walls of stone ever so high, ever so thick, reaching ever so far into the ground—there is a possibility that in some way or another I might be able to escape; but stand me on a floor and draw a chalk line around me and have me give my word of honor never to cross it. Can I get out of that circle? No, never! I'd die first."[6]

That quote made a deep impact on my youthful mind. It made me question what I would do if I was placed in that situation. It made me want to have integrity like Brother Maeser's throughout my daily life. It didn't always happen—I was far from perfect—but at least the desire was there and I tried to keep that quote in my mind as I went through all the rigors of teenhood.

My dad used to challenge all the children in my family to memorize certain poems he would pick out. He incentivized his challenge by telling us that for every poem we would memorize, he would give us a little cash for our hard work. As a little kid, this sounded like a sweet way to earn some candy money, and as I got older, a sweet way to earn some extra clothes money. So I accepted his challenge numerous times and I have never once regretted it. One of the first poems my dad ever gave me to memorize was a poem by the poet, Edgar A. Guest. It goes like this:

> Men talk too much of gold and fame,
> And not enough about a name;
> And yet a good name's better far
> Than all earth's glistening jewels are.
> Who holds his name above all price
> And chooses every sacrifice
> To keep his earthly record clear,
> Can face the world without a fear.
>
> Who never cheats nor lies for gain,
> A poor man may, perhaps, remain,
> Yet, when at night he goes to rest,
> No little voice within his breast
> Disturbs his slumber. Conscience clear,
> He falls asleep with naught to fear
> And when he wakes the world to face
> He is not tainted by disgrace.

Who keeps his name without a stain
Wears no man's brand and no man's chain;
He need not fear to speak his mind
In dread of what the world may find.
He then is master of his will;
None may command him to be still,
Nor force him, when he would stand fast,
To flinch before his hidden past.

Not all the gold that men may claim
Can cover up a deed of shame;
Not all the fame of victory sweet
Can free the man who played the cheat;
He lives a slave unto the last
Unto the shame that mars his past.
The only freedom here may own
Whose name a stain has never known.[7]

Before my dad would hand over the hard-earned cash for memorizing any poem, he would first have us recite the poem to him word for word. He would then ask us what we thought the meaning behind the poem was. It would always get us thinking because, if we didn't give some sort of answer, we wouldn't earn the full amount of money. We would end up having about a ten-minute discussion about the deeper meaning behind what we had just memorized. I think my dad was hoping that the values inside the poems he introduced to us would somehow grow deep into our hearts and become a part of us rather than being just a conglomeration of rhyming words that we knew by heart.

I can't speak for my brothers and sisters, but it definitely worked for me! All throughout my adolescent years I would think about these poems and recite them to myself. All throughout the challenging teen years I would have words such as these running through my head and they are what helped to fashion my decisions and helped to form my character—who I am today. Even now, years later, I still have these poems running through my head—as I wash the dishes, drive my car, run on the treadmill, and fold laundry. The best part is that I'm able to teach them to my children with the hopes that the high ideals contained within these poems will grow within their hearts as they did in mine, and bless their lives forever.

We need to surround our kids with goodness, with high and noble thoughts, continually! Our children are surrounded on a daily basis by movie stars, music idols, athletes, and kids at school, who teach them that to be cool and popular they need to dispense with their outdated morals. They teach our children that disrespect is funny, dishonesty gets you what you want, intelligence is for nerds, and chastity is for the ugly. We need to counteract those lies by teaching our children why morals are indispensable to a happy life. And how, by keeping them, it will greatly benefit their lives and the lives of others forever.

Everything that is good in this life makes its beginning from one tiny little action. An artistic masterpiece begins by just one stroke of the brush being swiped upon a canvas. A kingly redwood begins by just a single tiny seed being planted in moist and fertile soil. And a musical masterpiece first makes its beginnings with a single note being written on a musical staff. So it is with the morality of a nation. It begins with just one. If just one determined mother makes it her life's mission to instill within the souls of her children the beauties and virtues of integrity and moral courage, then as her children grow and blossom, they will affect all those within their sphere of influence for good—their children, their schoolmates, their coworkers, their church associates. And like dominoes, they will go on to affect the lives of all those *they* associate with. Throughout generations. Imagine if a multitude of mothers made it their life's work. The effect would be astronomical! It would change our nation. It could literally change the world!

REFERENCES

1. Gordon B. Hinckley, *Standing for Something: 10 Neglected Virtues That Will Heal Our Hearts and Homes* (New York: Times Books, 2000), 143.

2. Gordon B. Hinckley, *Standing for Something: 10 Neglected Virtues That Will Heal Our Hearts and Homes* (New York: Times Books, 2000), xxi.

3. Tobin Grant, "The Great Decline: 61 Years of Religiosity in One Graph,

2013 Hits a New Low" (presentation, Great Decline: Religion News Service, January 27 2014, http://religionnews.com/2014/01/27/great-decline-religion-united-states-one-graph/).

4. Gordon B. Hinckley, *Standing for Something: 10 Neglected Virtues That Will Heal Our Hearts and Homes* (New York: Times Books, 2000), xviii.

5. Margaret Thatcher in Gordon B. Hinckley, *Standing for Something: 10 Neglected Virtues That Will Heal Our Hearts and Homes* (New York: Times Books, 2000), xviii.

6. Karl G. Maeser in Gordon B. Hinckley, *Standing for Something: 10 Neglected Virtues That Will Heal Our Hearts and Homes* (New York: Times Books, 2000), 27.

7. Edgar A. Guest, "A Good Name," *Collected Verse of Edgar Guest* (1934).

MOMS WHO TEACH

"We can give our children education, lessons, athletics, the arts, and material possessions, but if we do not give them faith in Christ, we have given little."
—KEVIN W. PEARSON[1]

I had a pretty embarrassing family growing up. At least in my youthful mind I did. For as far back as I can remember, my family held family home evening not once a week like a "normal" Mormon family but *every single night* of the week! The embarrassing part for me as a youth was whenever I had non-member friends over, which, living in Southern California, was frequently. My friend and I would be hanging out in the house, doing our thing, when from seemingly out of nowhere there would be a sudden blast from our house intercom system with one of my parents shouting, "Everyone come down for family scripture time!" Without fail, they would make sure specifically to invite, by name, whichever friend was visiting the house that evening. The most embarrassing part of the whole situation was the tradition my parents invented. If ever there was a guest at the house, it was tradition that they be the one asked to say the prayer. Member and non-member alike. We heard some pretty interesting prayers throughout the years because of this tradition!

Despite my embarrassment, I started to notice something that I wasn't expecting at all. It seemed as though all of my friends, *especially* my non-member friends, would want to hang out at my house rather

129

than at their own. And when the time came for family home evening to start, every time without fail my friends were more than happy to join in. They actually thought it was *fun*, or maybe they just thought it was *funny* . . . either way, they always wanted to be a part of it. While I usually sat somewhat embarrassed during these family gatherings, my friends would be smiling and participating. They would not only say the "traditional" prayer (usually holding back laughter) but they would many times actually take a turn reading in the scriptures with my family! The more and more my friends joined in throughout the years, the less and less embarrassed I became. Strangely enough, during high school I actually thought it was cool to have new friends come in and join. Many times, I would wonder to myself what made my friends want to hang out at my house so much when they had to spend a large chunk of the time reading scriptures with my crazy family. The more and more I thought about it, the more I began to realize that my friends *craved* what I took for granted. They craved being a part of a strong and loving family. They craved having parents that actually cared enough to sit down with the family and teach them how to win at life. And, above all, I think they craved feeling the Spirit, something that was very foreign to many of my friends.

As humiliating as it was in the eyes of a young and immature pre-teen girl, now, as an adult looking back, I hold those times with my family sacred and know beyond all doubt that those experiences were the starting foundation of my testimony.

Gathering six children together of various ages and actually trying to have a lesson that brings in the Spirit is *not* an easy task! Especially if friends are added to the mix. But my parents made it a priority and stuck with it through the good and the bad. Our little family gatherings did not always turn out as my parents had hoped. Probably most of the time, actually! I remember numerous times when, instead of our meetings ending in prayer, they would end in a child or even sometimes a parent running out in tears or stomping off in anger. But still my parents persisted.

Elder Bednar and his wife, Susan, could definitely empathize with my parents:

Sometimes Sister Bednar and I wondered if our efforts to do these spiritually essential things were worthwhile. Now and then verses of scripture were read amid outbursts such as "He's touching me!" "Make him stop looking at me!" "Mom, he's breathing my air!" Sincere prayers occasionally were interrupted with giggling and poking. And with active, rambunctious boys, family home evening lessons did not always produce high levels of edification. At times Sister Bednar and I were exasperated because the righteous habits we worked so hard to foster did not seem to yield immediately the spiritual results we wanted and expected.

Today if you could ask our adult sons what they remember about family prayer, scripture study, and family home evening, I believe I know how they would answer. They likely would not identify a particular prayer or a specific instance of scripture study or an especially meaningful family home evening lesson as the defining moment in their spiritual development. What they would say they remember is that as a family we were consistent.[2]

I remember to this day many of the lessons my parents taught during those childhood family home evenings. I have actually used a number of them in lessons that I have taught throughout the years in Relief Society, Young Women, Primary, and of course with my own children. I probably remember them so well because my parents would repeat the same stories over, and over, and over, and over, again and again! How could I forget them, really? They were drilled into my brain! The lessons I remember the most are the personal stories told by my parents during our gatherings.

I remember my dad telling us a story of when he was a senior in high school and was at the Virginia state championships for wrestling. Anyone who knows anything about wrestling knows that there are specific weight divisions that the wrestlers are put in. Every time before a match, each wrestler is weighed-in to make sure that he is under the max weight limit for his division. If he is over—even by an ounce—he has to forfeit his match and he loses the points for his team. My dad had made it to the state championships his senior year. It was a two-day event where he would need to wrestle numerous challengers and beat them all in order to gain the title. He wrestled hard all throughout the first day of competition and beat every single one of his competitors. All he needed to do now was return the next day for the finals and beat one more wrestler to grab the title and become the Virginia state champion. He was so excited!

My dad enthusiastically entered the gymnasium the next morning and walked into the locker room to get weighed-in. As he stepped onto the cold scale, to my dad's utter horror, he was three pounds over his max limit! He would not be able to wrestle his final match for state champion! He was devastated. His whole team was devastated. The only way he would be able to wrestle was if he miraculously lost the weight before his match was to start. He had less than two hours to lose three pounds. His coach quickly hatched a plan to try and help him lose the weight. The coach turned the locker room showers on full blast at the hottest temperature, and the room quickly turned into a literal sweat locker. My dad dressed into two pairs of thick sweats to help make him sweat even more. He then ran around the steam-filled locker room while simultaneously spitting into the cup he was carrying. Every little bit he could get rid of helped! My dad ran like that for almost two hours. He finally exited the sweat box right before his match was to start and weighed himself to see if he made the cut. To everyone's astonishment, when my dad stepped onto the scale, he just made it. *Phew!* He would be able to wrestle his final match! He had just a few minutes before his match was to start and he literally felt like fainting. He had absolutely no energy left at all inside his body.

My dad's coach came over holding a little cup of tea for him to drink, hoping to put a little caffeine into my dad's system before the match. Drinking tea was against the Word of Wisdom, my dad knew that. But his coach kept pressuring him over and over again for him to drink it. My dad didn't know what to do. He had less than a few minutes before the match was to start, he had absolutely no energy for the match, and his coach was pressuring him to break the Word of Wisdom. Tough decision! My dad told his coach that he would be right back and quickly dashed into the steamy locker room again. He closed his eyes and said a quick prayer. He asked Heavenly Father if, in this unusual circumstance, he would be able to drink the tea to gain energy. My dad told us that an answer came immediately rushing to his head. He felt the words, "Craig, you have always kept the

Word of Wisdom. You shall run and not be weary, you shall walk and not faint." Those words pounded deeply into his questioning mind. Immediately, my dad walked out of the locker room, refused the tea that his coach was offering, and raced onto the black mat for his final championship match. Within a few moments my dad had his fierce competitor pinned firmly to the ground. The match was over. My dad was the new Virginia state champion in his weight division.

What kind of impression do you think that real-life story left on the minds of us children? I know what kind of impression it left on me! Do you think I ever even considered breaking the Word of Wisdom . . . even throughout my high school "peer pressure" years? Yeah, right! That decision was already firmly planted in my heart ever since I was little and I knew the power behind it. I knew I would never break my commitment to that goal after hearing that powerful experience from someone I trusted and loved so much.

Your stories don't need to be big, dramatic stories to be effective. Most of the stories my parents taught were simple, heartfelt stories of lessons they learned throughout their years of life. Frequently for family home evening my family would simply read a chapter of scripture and discuss the meaning behind it. On nights that were busier, my parents would pick out just one verse of scripture and we would discuss how it pertained to our own individual lives. Sometimes it seemed our lessons would last two hours and other times just ten minutes. The important thing is that my parents created a routine of spiritual education for their children and stuck with it! And it paid off with lasting, eternal dividends.

I remember little things that my parents would say and do during these family gatherings. Whenever we would have a family home evening where the Spirit was unusually strong, my parents would always point it out to the children by saying, "What you are feeling right now is the Spirit, remember this feeling." I did, and I still do. Another fond memory from these years were my mom's prayers. I remember dreading whenever it was my mom's turn to pray at the end of our gatherings. I knew my legs were going to go completely numb from lack of circulation for being in the kneeling position for so long. Her prayers (in my adolescent mind) were nearly the length of the movie *Pride and*

Prejudice . . . the six-hour BBC version! What's funny is seeing the same dread on my children's faces when I volunteer to pray. As soon as I volunteer, both of them will quickly shout out in synchronization, "Oh, that's alright, Mom, I'll say the prayer tonight." What am I going to say, "No"? I don't think so!

One memory that I know I will never forget happened one Sunday while I was sitting in my ten- or eleven-year-old primary class. My teacher asked all the children to raise their hands if they had ever heard their parents bear their testimonies before. My hand shot up like a rocket and in my head I was thinking, "Geez . . . my parents won't STOP bearing their testimonies to me . . . it's annoying!" I was literally about to fall off of my chair in disbelief when I looked out and saw that only one other kid—*one other*—in my large class had raised their hand. I couldn't believe it! That day, I gained a little bit more appreciation for my parents and their annoying testimony habits.

As mothers, God gives us permission to be annoying to our children. It's our duty! How many times do we hear almost the same exact talks given in general conference over and over again? All the time. Why? To drill the precepts into our heads! Why did the angel Moroni give almost the same exact message four separate times within one night to young Joseph? To drill it into his head. It's alright for us to do the same. One of the most effective teaching tools we have in our spiritual toolbox is our own life experiences. Good or bad. Children can learn just as much from your bad experiences than they can from your good. You have an expansive resource to pull from that will help your children learn the "why" of the gospel, not just the "what" of it. Tell your life stories to them and liken them to gospel principles. Explain to your children what you have learned from these experiences. That was the teaching method of our Savior when he lived on the earth. He would tell stories and then liken them to gospel principles, making the spiritual principles easier to grasp and easier to remember for the hearer.

Mothers, you don't need to wait for your husbands to gather the children together for these family study times. He may feel a little uncomfortable about it at first if his family didn't grow up having them. That's OK! Make it easy for him. Gather your children together, invite your husband—making sure to not do the "guilt-trip invite"—and I bet eventually he will be drawn in and start to really enjoy these times with the family.

As long as we are teaching our children with love, with the guidance of the Spirit, consistently, and with a little bit of fun added in every once in a while, our children will grow to appreciate the dedicated time and effort we spent teaching them and they will remember the lessons taught them when the challenging times arrive in their lives. They may forget them for a while or even rebel against them for a period, but the time will eventually come when, like Enos or Alma the younger, they will return to those teachings which brought fulfillment and happiness to their lives. They will remember the teachings of their mothers. What more can we ask for?

REFERENCES

1. Kevin Pearson, "Faith in the Lord Jesus Christ," *Ensign*, May 2009.
2. David A. Bednar, "More Diligent and Concerned at Home," *Ensign*, November 2009.

teach

BY

example

MOMS AS EXAMPLES

"What you do speaks so loud that I
cannot hear what you say."
—RALPH WALDO EMERSON[1]

As mothers, we have an extraordinary weight to bear. The magnitude of our parental duties may at times feel so overwhelming that we feel like hiding out in our closets, never to reappear. The reality of it is that who our children turn out to be to a large degree is all on us. We are our children's main source of what is acceptable or not, both in words and actions, until they leave our house. We have a few short years—that's it—to teach them through our examples, and then it's up to them whether to accept or reject the values and lessons we've tried to instill in them. Scary thought!

One of my favorite poets, Edgar A. Guest, penned these sobering words:

> There are little eyes upon you, and they're watching night and day;
> There are little ears that quickly take in every word you say;
> There are little hands all eager to do everything you do,
> And a little boy that's dreaming of the day he'll be like you.
>
> You're the little fellow's idol, you're the wisest of the wise;
> In his little mind about you no suspicions ever rise;
> He believes in you devoutly, holds that all you say and do
> He will say and do in your way when he's grown up just like you.

Oh, it sometimes makes me shudder when I hear my boy repeat
Some careless phrase I've uttered in the language of the street;
And it sets my heart to grieving when some little fault I see
And I know beyond all doubting that he picked it up from me.

There's a wide-eyed little fellow who believes you're always right,
And his ears are always open and he watches day and night;
You are setting an example every day in all you do
For the little boy who's waiting to grow up to be like you.[2]

Carol B. Hillman, a professor of early childhood education, once stated, "One of the most important things we adults can do for young children is to model the kind of person we would like them to be."[3] Our kids are like human sponges, soaking in everything we say and do. They may pretend like they don't pay attention to us, especially in the teen years, but it's all an act. They see all and hear all . . . and they catch on really quick when they see that we're not living up to the standards and principles we espouse to them on a daily basis. Our kids learn much more by our examples than they do by what we teach them. A mother can teach her child how to pray and teach her that prayer is important . . . but unless that child sees their mother in action, actually using prayer in her own life, it will mean little to the child.

I remember one experience I had while driving with my kids to a weekly music lesson. I'm usually really good about remembering to fasten my seatbelt while driving my car. But on this particular occasion, we were in a rush so I had mistakenly forgotten to buckle up before we raced off. As we were sweeping down the highway I asked my children if they had fastened their seatbelts. I quickly reminded them that if they hadn't done so yet, they better do it now! The next thing I heard coming from the back seat of my car was the little voice of my eight-year-old son pronouncing, "Mom, you're a hippo!" In shock I responded back, "What? Why would you call me a hippo, Trenton? That's not very nice." He then facetiously replied back to me, "Because you're a hypocrite! You don't even have your seatbelt on!" I then looked down and realized that he was right! I was driving unprotected without a seatbelt while simultaneously demanding them to put on theirs. I was being a hypocrite. At that moment, I regretted ever teaching my son that traitorous word! And I also realized that if we're teaching our children to follow rules that we don't follow or live up to ourselves, we might as well hang a neon sign over our heads with the word *HYPOCRITE* flashing in bold letters. At least that's what is flashing in the minds of our children at that precise moment! They won't be able to take us seriously. No mother wants to be caught off-guard being called a "hippo" by one of their children. Believe me, it was a little embarrassing!

As mothers, we're not only responsible for watching over the physical health and safety of our children but also, and more importantly, over the spiritual health and well-being of our children. One of the greatest tools we have in our parental toolbox for doing this is to show them *through our actions* what things are of greatest worth to us and what things should be avoided like the plague because of the harmful effects to both our physical and spiritual health. The things we allow into our lives are the things they will allow into their lives. The things we don't allow into our lives to a great extent are the things that they will stay away from as well. This, sadly, is not *always* the case. Our kids have their God-given agency and, as they get older, will choose for themselves. But there is a much greater chance they will keep with the good and stay away from the bad of the world if we have spent those crucial foundational years first gaining a close relationship with them and then exemplifying righteous behavior in both a physical and a spiritual sense.

My parents were great examples of this method of teaching by example. I remember countless times walking into my parents' bedroom before school and seeing my dad kneeling at the side of his bed pouring his heart out to God in prayer. He wasn't doing it for show or to teach me a lesson. He was all alone until I barged into his room. I would even get annoyed at times because I would need to talk to him about something I considered really important before I rushed off to school, but all I could do was sit there and twiddle my thumbs until he finally finished, which to my youthful mind seemed like an eternity!

I remember my mom literally spending all hours of the day and night—for years—preparing lessons for her seminary classes. She would read her scriptures constantly in order to be prepared for her six a.m. class the next morning. She would write music for each and every scripture mastery in order to help her students learn them easier. My mom gave her all to her calling and, although she wasn't doing it for the purpose of teaching me, through her consistent and unwavering example she was instructing me . . . and powerfully so. My parents weren't perfect examples, there is only one person who can claim that title. But the important thing is that they tried—really tried! That's all any of us are asked to do.

Conversely, while I was teaching my nine-year-old primary class a number of years ago, we got on the topic of listening to clean music and watching clean movies and television shows in order to keep the Spirit with us. One of my sweet little boys in class raised his hand and with a sort of embarrassed look on his face said, "My dad watches *really* bad movies with a *ton* of bad words in them! But at least he sends me and my sister to our rooms when he watches them. The only problem is that he turns the volume up so high that we can hear everything they're saying!" I still remember the sad look on his face when he announced this to the class. I felt a little uneasy about the situation. I definitely didn't want to put the child's father down, but at the same time, I also wanted to teach correct principles. We ended up using the rest of the class period talking about how the children should always strive to be good examples, sometimes even to their parents, just as their parents try to be good examples to them.

Kids should never have to be put into a situation where they feel like they need to exemplify good behavior in order to teach us, their parents, what's right. We need to strive to be a little more mindful of our daily words and actions and how they may affect our children's outlook on what's admissible.

My husband and I always talk about being careful not to have dog-poop brownies as a part of our metaphorical diet. Would any one of us mothers ever elect to eat a brownie that was offered to us if we were told just beforehand that it contained "just a little scoop of dog poop mixed into the batter"? Yeah right! Barf! But what if the giver assured us by saying, "Well, most of the brownie ingredients are good . . . there is just a tiny, a minuscule amount of dog poop mixed in. It should be fine." Would any of you eat it then? . . . Of course not! Then why do we sometimes elect to partake of media that contains less than desirable ingredients in them and teach our children through our examples that these things are worthwhile?

This is what Satan and the world sells to us and our children. Addictive dog-poop brownies that from the outside look so good and smell so amazing but as we bite into them, they are full of nasty germs that will pollute our bodies and ensnare the souls of our families.

Gene R. Cook, while speaking at Ricks College, told of a time when he sat conversing with Mick Jagger (lead singer for the Rolling Stones) for two hours during a flight to Dallas. Elder Cook recounts:

> After we visited back and forth a minute or two about what we were doing and all, I finally said something like, "You know, Mick, I have a question for you that I'd like you to answer for me." He said, "Well, I'll be glad to try." Then I said to him, "I have the opportunity to be with young people in many different places around the world, and some of them have told me that the kind of music you and others like you sing has no effect on them, that it's okay, and that it doesn't affect them adversely in any way. Then other young people have told me very honestly that your kind of music has a real effect on them for evil and that it affects them in a very bad way. You've been in this business for a long time, Mick. I'd like to know your opinion. What do you think is the impact of your music on the young people?"
>
> This is a direct quote, brothers and sisters. He said, "Our music is calculated to drive the kids to sex." . . . He quickly added, "Well, it's not my fault what they do. That's up to them. I'm just making a lot of money."[4]

As their conversation continued, Mick informed Elder Cook of more of his views saying:

> There is no God. There are no commandments. There are no rules, and thus you can do whatever you want. He told me of the importance, in his view, of freeing up the youth. He felt that they ought to be able to do whatever they wanted in spite of their parents. He said that parents were inhibiting them too much and controlling things and they ought not to be doing that. . . . He told me he was thankful the family, as an entity, was being destroyed. And I gathered from what he was saying that he was doing his best to help that along.[5]

Is this the kind of person we want influencing our children? We need to be fully aware of the mentors we place into the lives of our children, knowingly or unknowingly. Because truly they are mentors. If we hold these movie stars and music idols up on a pedestal, so will our children. If we listen to and watch their music and shows simply because we like the sound or overall storyline of it and ignore the obscene content contained within, whether we like it or not, that content is being stored in our body's computer filing system—our brain—and it adversely affects our thoughts, actions, and our ability to feel the Spirit. Satan disguises the "dog poop" to look and sound appealing. He will disguise it in a cool-sounding beat that catches your ear or in an interesting-looking show that catches your eye. But Satan's main goal is to ultimately capture your heart and mind with his deceptive lures until he has you addicted and you become a puppet in his hands. When our kids see us listening to and watching these things, they will follow suit, and it will act like a poison that slowly seeps into their once innocent hearts and minds, and they will slowly die to all things spiritual.

The Book of Mormon warns us, "Trust no one to be your teacher nor your minister, except he be a man of God, walking in his ways and keeping his commandments" (Mosiah 23:14).

I'm not trying to sound like an extremist here! I'm not saying that you should from now on only watch church movies that are approved by the men in suits or that you need to have the MoTab on repeat in your car. But I am saying that you should be more aware of the things you allow into your children's eyes, ears, and hearts . . . and into your own for that matter! In all aspects, be more aware. We need to pay closer attention to the movies we are watching, the music we are listening to, the way we speak *about* others, the way we speak *to* others, the way we treat others, how we handle disappointments, how we handle success, how we treat our callings, scripture study, prayer time, and the Sabbath day. The examples we set in each of these cases has great eternal significance in the lives of those we hold most dear—for they will most likely emulate our behavior whether good or bad.

Our children are like gardens that we as mothers tend. Our children start out as soil. Nice, pure, never-before-planted-in soil. Through the years of their early development, we are the gardener that fosters life in that fresh soil. We are in charge of adding the essential nutrients to their youthful soil. If we neglect our duties, our children's soil will become dry and barren dirt in which only weeds and dry brush can break through and grow. But, if we continually add life-giving nutrients to their soil and plant seeds of the most beautiful sort in their rich soil, as they grow, their souls will become a bounteous garden that will bless their lives and the lives of others forever. We decide what seeds will be planted in those early formative years. And as they mature, they will use our example as a guide to what seeds they will allow to be planted in their hearts in the future.

Our dear President Hinckley gives all of us hope for becoming better examples to our children when he counseled us to, "Try a little harder to be a little better."6 That's it! Try a little harder to be a better example tomorrow than you were today for your children. Then the next day do the same. And the next day. And so on. Gradually climbing up the ladder of discipleship one day at a time, one rung at a time. "Be thou an example of the believers, in word, in conversation, in charity, in spirit, in faith, in purity" (1 Timothy 4:12), for the sake of our innocent and precious children.

REFERENCES

1. Ralph Waldo Emerson, "Social Aims" (1875).
2. Edgar A. Guest, "His Example," *Collected Verse of Edgar Guest* (1934).
3. Carol B. Hillman, www.quotehd.com/quotes/carol-b-hillman-one-of-the-most-important-things-we-adults-can-do-for-young-children.
4. Gene R. Cook, "The Eternal Nature of the Law of Chastity," (presentation, Ricks College, Rexburg, ID, 1989, abish.byui.edu/reserve/E_Cook_Chastity_Talk.pdf).
5. Ibid.
6. Gordon B Hinckley, "We Have Work To Do," *Ensign*, May 1995.

MOMS WHO ARE IN TUNE

"Yea, behold, I will tell you in your mind and in your heart, by the Holy Ghost, which shall come upon you and which shall dwell in your heart. Now, behold, this is the spirit of revelation."
—D&C 8:2-3

I had an experience shortly after I was married, which taught me just how important it is for all mothers to learn how to receive, recognize, and respond to the promptings of the Holy Ghost. The experience I will relate was not trumpeted to my ears by a booming voice from the heavens above nor was it a time when I was secretly visited by a heavenly messenger. Those experiences have never happened to me! Rather, the experience came to me at a time when my mind was quiet and receptive, allowing the Holy Ghost to penetrate the innermost depths of my mind with a message that needed to be heard right away.

In 2005, Greg and I were just newly married and living in Springville, Utah. He was working with a contractor laying tile flooring and I was working as a preschool teacher at a tiny school in Provo called Adventure Time. One afternoon at work, I was just getting the last of my little preschoolers to sleep for their routine midday nap. After the last child had finally fallen asleep, I quietly tiptoed over to a corner of the darkened room, where a tiny ray of sunlight slipped through the paper shades covering the two large windows in the front of the elongated classroom.

As I sat there excitedly reading my newly purchased *Harry Potter and the Half-Blood Prince* in the corner of the room, a silent thought entered my mind.

"Move Aurora" was all that it said.

Aurora was one of my little preschoolers who was sleeping soundly on her little mat across the room from where I was reading. I immediately blew off the notion, wondering *why in the world* I would think such a random thought. There was no way that I was going to move any of the children and chance waking them up from their much-needed naps and, not to mention, my much-needed break!

I continued reading until the thought entered my mind again, "Move Aurora."

Again, I questioned my sanity, thinking, "Yeah, right . . . she just barely fell asleep! If I move her now, she will wake up and then all the kids will wake up. Nap time will be over and I won't be able to read my new book! There is *not a chance!*"

I continued reading until, for a third and final time, I felt the words "Move Aurora" enter my mind.

This time, feeling like this was really out of the ordinary, so it must be something important, I decided that I should probably listen. I stood up, grabbed Aurora's little blue foam mat and pulled her across the carpeted room. After moving her, I sat back down in my small corner and again commenced reading *Harry Potter*.

What seemed like just moments after I had moved Aurora from her place on the carpet, the large clock that had been hanging on the wall just over her head came crashing down to the ground and shattered into a million sharp fragmented pieces! All at once, the children shot up like torpedoes from their sleeping mats, total shock and confusion painted on their formerly comatose expressions.

I learned four things right then and there.

First, I learned that nap time was most assuredly over.

Second, I learned that God loves Aurora more than she will ever know.

Third, I learned that we are God's hands here on earth to do His work.

Lastly, I learned that I need to not question myself but act when a prompting first enters my mind.

President Boyd K. Packer taught, "Each of us must stay in condition to respond to inspiration and the promptings of the Holy Ghost. The Lord has a way of pouring pure intelligence into our minds to prompt us, to guide us, to teach us, and to warn us. Each son or daughter of God can know the things they need to know instantly."[1]

What a comfort this should be to all mothers!

There has never been a time on this earth where the need has been greater for mothers to know how to receive, recognize, and respond to the promptings of the Holy Ghost as the day in which we live right now! Satan knows the end is nigh and is dispatching his forces day and night to blind the eyes and darken the minds of the precious spirits God has entrusted to us. But the good news is that God has not left us alone in this sacred calling of motherhood! Of course He wouldn't! He has a vested interest in our success as mothers. After all, they are His children too! God has given us the perfect guide to help us steer His children down the paths that will bring them safely home. All we need to do is learn how to utilize this divine gift.

Elder Bednar once stated, speaking to a group of college students that, "*Prayer* is the process whereby we as sons and daughters communicate with our Heavenly Father . . . *revelation* is the process whereby Heavenly Father communicates with us" (italics added). If revelation is how God speaks to his children, then it's probably pretty crucial for us to learn how to understand what He is trying to tell us![2]

I know this is a stretch, but imagine this: you are in command of a small army unit. You think your unit is safe hiding out in the fortifications where you are stationed. Little do you know, spies have informed the enemy of your exact location and where the precise weaknesses are in your fortifications. They are on the move to attack. Your top general knows the situation and is personally trying to contact you to warn you of the imminent danger. But there's a problem: your line of communication is down and you are unable to receive the warning from your general. It doesn't look too hopeful for your unit, does it?!

Each of us mothers *are* in command of a small unit—your family! We have our fortifications—our homes—where we are stationed. The other side knows exactly where each one of your family members are located at all times and, on top of that, knows all their weaknesses. Our

Heavenly Father knows the situation our families are in; He knows of the dangers that surround us daily. Often, He tries to contact us through the Holy Ghost, who acts as His messenger, His line of communication, to warn us of imminent threats to our family's physical health as well as spiritual health . . . but are we listening? Do we know how to read the messages? Is our line of communication down?

My son, Trenton, has been playing the violin for a little over a year now. Every time he meets with his teacher for a lesson, the first thing they do is tune his violin. Not only is it the first thing they do, but it's the *most important* thing they do throughout the whole lesson! The reason is obvious, of course. It wouldn't matter how many angelic songs my son learned nor would it matter how masterfully he played them if he did not *first* spend the time and effort tuning his violin. The music would sound off pitch and be very painful to the ear if he neglected this initial step.

His teacher begins the tuning process by holding up a metal tuning fork. He then knocks it gently on his knee to start it vibrating. This particular tuning fork rings in the pure and constant pitch of the A string on Trenton's violin. His teacher then proceeds to tune each individual string to the pitch of the vibrating tuning fork. Making each string perfectly in tune with the others. When completed, Trenton is then asked to match his voice to the pitch of the fork. This same process has gone on for a little over a year now. As time has gone on, it has become much easier for Trenton to pick out an A pitch whenever he hears one being played on an instrument or on the radio because he has worked to commit it to memory. The more he has worked on recognizing the pure and true ring of the tuning fork, the faster he has been able to recognize it when he hears its melodic voice again.

Speaking of this same process, Elder Bednar stated: "A tuning fork provides a constant standard or pitch to which a musical instrument is tuned. Just like the sound produced by [a] tuning fork, the Holy Ghost is constant, steady, and sure. The sound is not brash like the crashing of symbols; it is not loud like the sound of a trumpet. It is subtle and subdued; it whispers and beckons in softness. And you and I must tune the strings of our souls to the standard of the Holy Ghost."[3]

President Faust used a similar metaphor when teaching about the voice of the Spirit. He compared the Holy Ghost to a *channel* that we need to attune ourselves to. Think of one of those old-time radios. One of the radios with a knobby tuning dial. Imagine we are trying to listen to a specific channel—say for instance, 89.7. As we turn the dial to find the channel we desire, what are we likely to hear? Well, more than likely we will hear voices from talking heads that we were not searching for, we would probably hear music from other channels that we were not looking to listen to, or we may even hear earsplitting static, like nails on a chalkboard, grating at our eardrums. We would hear everything except what we were looking for, until, finally, we hit 89.7 on the dial, the station we were searching for all along. As we slowly approach closer and closer to our intended channel, we start to hear bits and pieces of the message along with the static. The nearer we get, the clearer the message becomes.

President Faust spoke of this:

> There are so many kinds of voices in the world that compete with the voice of the Spirit. The Spirit's voice is ever present, but it is calm. The adversary tries to smother this voice with a multitude of loud, persistent, persuasive, and appealing voices: Murmuring voices that conjure up perceived injustices. Whining voices that abhor challenge and work. Seductive voices that offer sensual enticements. Soothing voices that lull us into carnal security. Intellectual voices that profess sophistication and superiority. Proud voices that rely on the arm of flesh. Flattering voices that puff us up with pride. Cynical voices that destroy hope. Entertaining voices that promote pleasure seeking. And commercial voices that tempt us to "spend money for that which is of no worth, and our labor for that which cannot satisfy.[4]

Satan's strategy? Jam the circuits. Overload the lines of communication with meaningless and endless chatter. We have become totally and completely addicted to this chatter. We are literally surrounded by chatterboxes everywhere we go. Chatter from our smartphones, chatter from our TVs, chatter from our radios—just to name a few. Even our watches are beginning to talk to us. We can't have family time, run errands, or go on vacation without receiving text messages, junk mail, or push notifications every five to ten seconds! The chatter is constant and it follows us wherever we go. It's almost as if people become anxious if there isn't some sort of incessant noise blaring in their eardrums every moment of every day. They feel as though they are missing out on some life-changing piece of information or something. We have become as the Athenians of old that the apostle Paul spoke of when he said of them, "For all the Athenians and strangers which were there spent their time in nothing else, but either to tell, or to hear some new thing" (Acts 17:21).

President Faust continues:

> I suggest a simple solution for selecting the channel to which we attune ourselves: listen to and follow the voice of the Spirit. This is an ancient solution, even eternal, and may not be popular in a society that is always looking for the new. It requires patience in a world that demands instant gratification. This solution is quiet, peaceful, and subtle in a world enamored by that which is loud, incessant, fast paced, garish, and crude. This solution requires you to be contemplative while your peers seek physical titillation. This solution is one unified, consistent, age-old message in a world that quickly becomes bored in the absence of intensity, variety, and novelty. This solution requires us to walk by faith in a world governed by sight. We need to learn how to ponder the things of the Spirit and to respond to its promptings—to filter out the static generated by Satan. As we become attuned to the Spirit, we shall hear a word behind us, saying, 'This is the way, walk ye in it.' Hearkening to the voice of the living God will give us peace in this world, and eternal life in the world to come. These are the greatest of all the gifts of God.[5]

So, how can we learn to attune ourselves to the voice of the Spirit? How can we gain the ability to *know* what God would have us know at the very moment we need it? Elder Bednar speaks of four basic principles, that if followed, will greatly enhance our ability to receive and recognize these subtle promptings in our daily lives.

The very first principle is to *desire* the companionship of the Holy Ghost.[6]

Desire is somewhat of a nebulous term. I can say that I have a desire for a delicious and juicy Chick-fil-A sandwich, but if I don't go out to my car, drive to the store, order it, and pay the money for it . . . then how badly do I actually desire it? Not very badly, I would have to say.

If we truly have a desire to have this divine gift working in our lives throughout the day, then we need to put in the effort to be able to receive and worthy to receive this priceless gift.

We need to get rid of the clutter in our lives. Not the physical clutter like the knick-knacks laying around our houses, but the things that clutter up our minds with nonsense.

I try to be a pretty decent house keeper. I like to have everything neat and tidy. The carpets vacuumed on a regular basis, the furniture neatly dusted. But for some strange reason, it seems like I never have enough time in the day to clean out my bedroom closet. Clutter is everywhere! Piles of clutter—clothes, shoes, hangers, Saran Wrap–looking bags that came from my husband's dry-cleaned suits from months before. Yeah, it's pretty bad.

It seems that whenever I'm needing to rush off to run an errand, I can never find the clothes I'm looking for to get dressed in. They are laying somewhere in the jumbled mess on my floor. I spend minutes and minutes searching for that one item I am trying to find, but in the disaster of my closet, it might as well be in a black hole—there's no way I'm finding it. So, finally I end up just throwing on whatever is sitting on top of the pile of cluttered clothes.

Similarly, clutter of the mind makes it nearly impossible for us to receive or recognize the voice of the Spirit. If there is too much stuff of little value being ingested into the diet of your mind, it will block out or hide the items of greatest value. Turn off the things that your mind is consuming that have little to no nutritional value to them and show God that your deepest desire is to be filled with things that are of greatest worth. Clean out and declutter your mind and He will fill it.

The second principle Elder Bednar gives is to *invite* the companionship of the Holy Ghost.[7]

My grandpa was an aeronautical engineer at McDonnell Douglas—an aerospace manufacturing corporation—for many, many years. He was assigned to design the cooling system to be used in the Apollo Spacecraft missions, including Apollo 11—whose mission it was to be the first manned spacecraft to the moon and back. My mom once asked him how he was able to accomplish such an amazing feat.

My grandpa's reply was, "I didn't."

He continued:

> I was so concerned and worried about getting this right since people's lives were at stake—not to mention millions of dollars—that I knew I couldn't do it alone. It was beyond my human capabilities. So I did what I do every time I face an unconquerable mountain. *I prayed fervently, seeking guidance and enlightenment from the Lord* before I went to bed.
>
> In the middle of the night I was awakened by my thoughts. The Lord revealed to me how the system should be constructed. I got out of bed in the pitch-black night while everyone else in the house was asleep and drew in my work notebook exactly what was shown to me in my mind.[8]

After that night, he was able to bring his drawings to work and have the design team put their work together to create a mock up that eventually became the cooling system that was used in the Apollo 11 rocket.

My grandpa was able to fulfill his daunting assignment through the inspiration of the Lord—because he first was willing to ask the Lord for His guidance and then had faith that he would receive the answer.

Elder Bednar explains, "We receive more readily and recognize more clearly the influence of the Holy Ghost as we specifically invite Him into our lives."[9]

His third principle is to *heed* simple promptings.

He says, "We are prompted by the Holy Ghost every day to do ordinary and simple things. *To the degree* that we heed these simple promptings, then our capacity to recognize and respond to the Holy Ghost is increased. To the degree that we do not heed these simple promptings, then our capacity to recognize and respond to the Holy Ghost is decreased. We are either progressing or regressing in our ability to recognize and respond to the Holy Ghost. There is no neutral ground; there is no standing still."[10]

Speaking at General Conference on this subject, Elder Rasband stated, "We must be confident in our first promptings. Sometimes we rationalize; we wonder if we are feeling a spiritual impression or if it is just our own thoughts. When we begin to second-guess, even third-guess, our feelings—and we all have—we are dismissing the Spirit; we are questioning divine counsel. The prophet Joseph Smith taught that if you will listen to the first promptings, you will get it right nine out of ten times."[11]

The fourth and final principle is to heed the promptings *quickly*.[12] Elder Bednar stated:

> Have you ever received and recognized a prompting from the Holy Ghost, and then decided to respond to it "later"? And then when later arrived, you found that you could not remember the prompting. I have learned that acting upon promptings quickly greatly increases our capacity to receive and recognize the influence of the Holy Ghost.
>
> I have also learned that properly recording spiritual impressions demonstrates to the Savior how much I treasure His direction. The simple practice of writing down spiritual thoughts and feelings greatly enhances the likelihood of receiving and recognizing additional promptings from the Holy Ghost.[13]

I can't tell you how often within these past few months of writing this book that thoughts from out of nowhere would just pop into my mind. I was always ready and waiting with my phone's notepad so that I could type out the inspiration I received. It is honestly amazing to me how many more promptings I receive now that the Lord knows that my mind is opened wide and ready to receive.

Mothers, it is absolutely vital to the lives of our family members—each and every individual—that we learn how to receive this communication from God. Our children are each going to face times where their lives will be in imminent danger, just like my little preschooler, Aurora, was. Only it won't just be physical danger that is threatening them, but even scarier—spiritual danger. Many of the headaches and heartaches we will face as parents cannot be solved on our own, by our own intellect and wisdom. There are too many unseen traps set by Satan to trip up and capture our children, too many unknown factors that are hidden from our finite and limited vision that only God himself can see and know of.

God is eager to broaden the scope of our vision that we may know how to individually assist our children in their most desperate times of need. That we may know how to guide them around the pitfalls the enemy has prepared for their downfall. And that we may know precisely how to lovingly council them when they have been knocked down and are seemingly on the brink of spiritual death.

God knows perfectly the heart and mind of each and every one of His children. He knows how they can be reached even when we feel there is little hope left. He will inspire us to do things and say things that we normally wouldn't think to do or say that can—little by little—help to break apart the hardened outer layers of our children's hearts, leaving the softened penetrable layers open to be pricked by the Holy Ghost. We are *never ever* alone in raising our children. Truly, God is our wisest and most faithful companion in this heart-wrenching privilege we have of guiding God's children in this mortal sphere. All we need do is put in the effort of learning how to receive and recognize the promptings of the Holy Spirit.

REFERENCES

1. Boyd K. Packer, "These Things I Know," *Ensign*, May 2013.
2. David A. Bednar, "Receiving, Recognizing, and Responding to the Promptings of the Holy Ghost" (devotional given at Ricks College, Rexburg, ID, August 31, 1999, www2.byui.edu/Presentations/Transcripts/Devotionals/1999_08_31_Bednar.htm).
3. Ibid.
4. James E Faust, "Voice of the Spirit," *Ensign*, June 2006.
5. Ibid.
6. David A. Bednar, "Receiving, Recognizing, and Responding to the Promptings of the Holy Ghost" (devotional given at Ricks College, Rexburg, ID, August 31, 1999, www2.byui.edu/Presentations/Transcripts/Devotionals/1999_08_31_Bednar.htm).
7. Ibid.
8. Vicky Burnham, in discussion with the author, October 2017.
9. David A. Bednar, "Receiving, Recognizing, and Responding to the Promptings of the Holy Ghost" (devotional given at Ricks College,

Rexburg, ID, August 31, 1999, www2.byui.edu/Presentations/Transcripts
/Devotionals/1999_08_31_Bednar.htm).

10. Ibid.

11. Ronald A. Rasband, "Let the Holy Spirit Guide," *Ensign*, May 2017.

12. David A. Bednar, "Receiving, Recognizing, and Responding to the Promptings of the Holy Ghost" (devotional given at Ricks College, Rexburg, ID, August 31, 1999, www2.byui.edu/Presentations/Transcripts
/Devotionals/1999_08_31_Bednar.htm).

13. Ibid.

MOMS WHO PREPARE

"If I had eight hours to chop down a tree,
I'd spend six hours sharpening the ax."
—ABRAHAM LINCOLN[1]

I want to take a minute and focus on the young women who are in the crucial preparatory stages of motherhood. Although, if you're already a seasoned mom, keep reading, this will be good for you too!

You amazing young women have your whole lives ahead of you; this is an exciting time of life you are in! With each passing day, the choices you make right now, day by day, good or bad, are the building blocks for your future life and determine to a large extent who you'll become as adults.

These are pivotal years in your life. I remember being your age; I thought time dragged on and on at a snail's pace. I remember when I was in elementary school, I couldn't wait until I would be old enough to enter middle school with my cool older siblings that I looked up to so much. When I finally made it to middle school, high school seemed like it would never come! And when I finally made it to high school, marriage and children seemed like a far distant dream. But here I am, married with two children, and I am wondering where the time has gone. Looking back, those twenty or so years of preparatory time flew by like a blink of an eye. It's crazy to me!

I had a pretty unusual two years of prep time shortly before I became a mother. Just preceding these two years of prep, I was living my life as a normal young adult, attending school down by the beach, having fun with friends in the Huntington Beach singles ward, dating, going to church dances, blasting my Biggy Smalls album out the sun roof of my car and thinking that I was pretty cool and that life was really good!

Then something happened. I met my future husband, Greg, one Sunday at the singles ward and that's when my life changed . . . for the better, of course! To make a very long and interesting story short, I met my future husband right when he was on the brink of trying to decide whether to go on a mission or keep with his plan of continuing on with his college baseball career. Through a series of spiritual experiences, the decision was finally made that Greg would go on a mission and drop his baseball scholarships and potential pro-ball career. The following months before he left on his mission were filled with both Greg and I working together to help prepare him for his mission. We studied the scriptures and other gospel-related books continually, attended insti- tute classes, went to church and firesides together, we would even go on dates to evangelical book stores and hide their anti-Mormon literature. Yeah . . . we were weird.

If you can believe it, right before he left on his mission he proposed to me, and I said "yes" . . . crazy, right? A couple months later, Greg flew off to Michigan for two years and I remained in California with a ring on my finger. (Just a little side note for any of you young ladies out there . . . I don't recommend what we did for everyone, but we received a witness that it was the right thing for us, so we followed the prompting.)

Throughout the two years while he was gone, I focused not only on my job and schooling like any normal person my age, but more impor- tantly, I focused on growing spiritually. I knew Greg was going to be growing a ton while on his mission and I didn't want him to come home and be on a higher level of spirituality than me. Therefore, I set goals throughout this time that I felt would help me grow in like manner. My two main spiritual goals would be to read my scriptures each and every day and say more meaningful and heartfelt prayers daily.

As the months passed, a very interesting and unexpected thing started to happen as I kept up with my goals each day. Reading my scriptures no longer became a thing I had to do to keep up on my goal. I actually yearned to read my scriptures. Every moment of free time I had, whether I was at school, on my lunch break at work, at the gym, or at my house, I had my scriptures with me and I was devouring them. As odd as it sounds, I actually felt like they had become my best friends. I probably sound like a total loser now but it's true!

During this time, other interesting things started happening to me. I began to pray not out of obligation, but because I desired to converse with my Father in Heaven in whom I felt a growing bond with. Also, I slowly began to notice that the music I used to listen to made me feel sick inside, empty and dark. I could actually physically feel the light of the Spirit diminish in me when I was listening to it. So I turned the jams off and replaced them with music that was uplifting to my soul . . . sorry, Big Papa!

Same with many of the television shows and movies I used to watch. I couldn't watch them anymore; they irked me. It's not like I even watched horrible, pornographic shows or anything. The shows I used to watch were just shallow and pointless time-wasters to me now. Where I was once desensitized to the things that would take the Spirit away from me . . . I became sensitized to them again. And I loved it! I never felt so good in my life. I felt like there was a perpetual warmth glowing inside my body that made me feel truly happy. I also started receiving inspiration daily and seeing true miracles happen in my life. It was amazing!

As I began to grow more sensitive to the promptings of the Spirit, I began to see characteristics within myself that I knew I needed to change in order to become more pure and clean in the eyes of God. It's very interesting how the Spirit works. It felt as if most of my life was lived looking in a foggy mirror at myself, not quite being able to see the dirty smudges on my face that needed washing off. But as I grew closer to my Father in Heaven, the fog began to lift from the mirror and I was able to see for the first time what needed cleansing, and I had the pure faith that I could do it with the Savior's help.

One such example is when I prayed two evenings in a row, pleading with God to help me know if my mind was too focused on the things of this world. Was I too fixated on what the world considers beauty rather than what the Lord considers beauty? Did I waste too much of my precious God-given time working on my outward appearance rather than on my inward?

I loved working out, I always have. I was kind of obsessed with it. And I would usually work out intensely two times a day. Before I go any further, I'm not wanting to paint the impression that I'm saying exercise is bad. Of course it's not bad, we need to take care of these bodies that God has given us. But what *is* bad and what I felt personally about myself—and what I know the Spirit was also revealing to me—was the fact that I was *not* working out for the main purpose of being healthy and active. I was working out so much because I was striving to look like the impossible images on the magazine covers, the false idols of the world.

Those were the questions I brought to the Lord that I was seeking an answer for. I asked Him to show me some sort of sign that would help me know for sure that I should chill out with my workouts and focus that time on more important things. Now I must warn you that when you fervently ask God for an answer, He will always answer you in one way or another . . . sometimes in ways that you're least expecting.

God gave me my answer the day following my second prayer. I had been at a missionary council meeting because I was a ward missionary, and after the meeting I drove straight to the gym like I always did. On my way home from the gym, a man on his cell phone ran a red light just as I was turning left at a main intersection. He smashed my car to pieces, literally: it was completely totaled. Although I wasn't wearing a seatbelt at the time (not smart), I walked away with just a broken ankle. Just enough injury to keep me from going to the gym for a few months. Just enough time to help me kick my obsessive addiction.

It was my answer. I knew it immediately! I was actually smiling on the gurney in the middle of the intersection as they placed me in the ambulance. After I was secured in the ambulance, one of the paramedics asked me if I needed anything from my car before they drove off. I quickly asked if they could retrieve my scriptures for me. They probably thought I was a little weird asking for my scriptures rather than, you know, important stuff like my purse or shoes, but my scriptures were all I could think about. I couldn't lose them!

Many life-changing miracles branched off of that one answer to my fervent prayer as well as the knowledge that God is present in our lives. He is seeking to refine us and to make us more than we are if we will allow Him to. He will shield us from the temptations and flattery of Satan and help us become "new creatures" if we will prove that we are dedicated and faithful to Him through our consistent actions.

Our Heavenly Father desires to help us in all aspects of our lives because He loves us and wants to see us become our full potential as His daughters. Satan also desires to have us. Not because he cares for us in the least, but because he is set on seeing us fail. He revels in the failure of others. If you don't believe me, open up your Pearl of Great Price to the book of Moses, chapter 7. In this chapter, the prophet Enoch is being shown a vision. In the vision he sees Satan, and the scripture says, "He beheld Satan; and he had a great chain in his hand, and it veiled the whole face of the earth with darkness; and he looked up and laughed, and his angels rejoiced" (Moses 7:26). Seriously?! That's one evil dude.

One of the most profound scripture passages of all time is the story of Lehi's dream. It shows precisely how Satan has been working in the lives of men and women, girls and boys, throughout the ages to destroy them. As in the earlier scripture, it describes Satan's mist of darkness that he uses to blind the eyes of us all. Blind us from the knowledge of who we truly are. Blind us from the knowledge of what our true potential is. Blind us from the only true path that will lead us to lasting happiness.

Along with the mist, he sets up many counterfeit paths and tricks people into thinking that they can walk down any path they prefer and happiness will inevitably be found. When in reality, all they will find is regret and misery at the end of the road.

He also sets up false gods for people to worship so that they won't have the time or the desire to worship the one true God. These people he sets high up in the air like stars, above the mist of darkness, so that people are sure to see them. As it states in 1 Nephi 8, "I beheld . . . a great and spacious building; and it stood as it were in the air, high above the earth. And it was filled with people, both old and young, both male and female; and their manner of dress was exceedingly fine; and they were in the attitude of mocking and pointing their fingers towards those who had come at and were partaking of the fruit" (1 Nephi 8:26–27).

These manufactured "gods" of Satan are the celebrities of music, movies, sports, TV, YouTube, and magazines that you can't help but see everywhere you go, unless you live in a bubble or something. We do not want to be like them! They are not happy. Fame, fortune, and popularity is not what makes a happy life. It is what many times destroys a life. I can give a huge list of "stars" who found misery in that great and spacious building and not happiness. The glitter of the building is false advertising.

Satan is pounding so hard on you, trying to turn your gaze away from that which will bring true and lasting happiness. He knows that if he can get you off course, then he can get generations off course. Don't let him! You have a responsibility to yourself as well to your future children to put in the effort and do what it takes to become what Elder Russell M. Nelson calls "sin-resistant."[2] It is important to note that there is no such thing as "sin-proof" here on earth. You can't consistently surround yourself with music, with media, with people, with events that will harm your soul and expect that none of it will affect you. Inevitably, those things which would injure you spiritually will end up rubbing off on you if you don't watch what you do and who you surround yourself with.

I'm not saying that you should live your life like a nun in a convent. Of course not! You should go out and have fun with friends, date good guys, and experience a full life. All I'm saying is that as you put your full effort into truly gaining a relationship with Christ and as you immerse yourself in the words of the prophets; as you pray earnestly to your Heavenly Father throughout your day and have your thoughts focused more and more on Him, you will start to desire different things than you once did. You will start to feel as the people in King Benjamin's day felt when they cried out, "The Spirit of the Lord, which has wrought a mighty change in us; or in our heart, that we have *no more disposition to do evil,* but to do good continually" (Mosiah 5:2; italics added).

You will be re-sensitized rather than desensitized to the things that surround you each day and you will be better able to recognize what things are spiritually harmful for you to be around throughout your day. You will be better able to feel the promptings of the Spirit because you will be a purer vessel than you once were. You will literally have a spiritual protective layering surrounding you at all times . . . as long as you keep it up.

You will truly be sin-resistant and you will know how to teach your future children to be sin-resistant as well. You will be as a female Captain Moroni, when it says of him, "If all men [and women] had been, and were, and ever would be, like unto Moroni, behold, the very powers of hell would have been shaken forever; yea, *the devil would never have power over the hearts of the children of men*" (Alma 48:17; italics added). Wow! Now that's true and lasting power!

President Boyd K. Packer made this bold statement, "The Lord is voting for me and Lucifer is voting against me, but it is my vote that counts."[3] So what will it be? Who do you choose to follow? Who do you choose to become?

REFERENCES

1. Abraham Lincoln, http://wiki.c2.com/?SharpenTheSaw.
2. Russell M. Nelson, "A Plea to My Sisters," *Ensign*, November 2015.
3. Boyd K. Packer, "Cleansing the Inner Vessel," *Ensign*, November 2010.

MOMS WHO WAGE WAR

"The only thing necessary for the triumph of evil is that good men [and women] do nothing."
—EDMUND BURKE[1]

I was *starving!* I mean, not literally . . . but I was definitely needing *something* in my belly to stop it from eating itself! My kids and I had just finished school and I had not had the chance to eat anything *all day*. Fortunately, my all-knowing sister knew my pain, so she invited us over to try the new sushi restaurant that had just opened up by her house. Since sushi is the greatest invention of all human history, there was *no way* I was going to turn down her generous offer. My two kids and I hopped in our car and raced over to meet my sister and her three little kids at the restaurant. As we walked in, we could see that huge TV screens lined the walls on each side of us. We were completely surrounded by them. We didn't think much of it at the time and sat down and began looking at our menus.

As the time passed and we were awaiting our food, I looked around at the children. Can you guess what they were doing? Of course . . . their eyes were glazed over, staring at the enormous TV screens. Football was playing and the children were enjoying watching the teams battle it out. The perfect little babysitters as we sat there waiting.

My sister and I sat conversing, having a great time, when from out of my peripheral vision, I saw my innocent six-year-old son, like a flash, look away from the screen that had moments before captivated his gaze. I looked over at him to see what was wrong and he had a look of complete embarrassment on his face. I glanced up at the screens to see what would put such a look on my tiny son's face, and what I saw put a look of embarrassment on *my* face . . . as well as a look of extreme anger!

On every single TV screen in the restaurant, there were two almost totally nude girls, eating the newest Carl's Jr. sandwich creation. The commercial was trying to point out the fact that two slabs of meat were better than only one single slab of meat on a bun. To emphasize their point, they portrayed two other slabs of meat—the almost nude women—eating the two slabbed sandwiches. No wonder my sweet son felt awkward at that moment!

Greg and I have made sure over the years to teach both of our children about the lies that the world teaches about the female gender. We have also, from the earliest of ages, taught them simple truths—at their age level—about the destructive nature of pornography. Why at such an early age would we bother to teach them these things? Well, for moments such as these! Kids can't get away from crap like this anymore. It's everywhere they turn! My son knew that what he was seeing was wrong, even at his young age, so he quickly looked away in discomfort. I glanced over at my daughter, and she too had looked away, but not before viewing what the world defines as true womanhood. What a message for my daughter to learn as we sat there eating sushi. That she is a piece of meat, ready to be sold and consumed by salivating male customers. But that is not true.

Later that evening, when Greg came home from work, I told him what had happened at the restaurant. We both sat there disgusted at the negligent and scandalous way Carl's Jr. sought to entice people to purchase their food. To degrade and monetize one half of the population to stimulate and attract the other half of the population . . . great tactic!

The following day, Greg wrote an article on his blog on how destructive to the human psyche those commercials actually are. The blog post went completely viral. I guess there were others who felt as disgusted as we were . . . both in and out of the church! The result was a Twitter storm using the tag and Twitter handle @carlsjr. Every time someone tweeted Greg's blog, Carl's Jr. would be notified about it.[2]

Hundreds of thousands of both men and women joined together to make a stand. Boycotts ensued, and just recently, Carl's Jr. pulled all their pornographic ads, declaring that the advertising just wasn't working anymore.[3]

I truly believe that this was made possible because an army of moms who were trying to protect their families from this evil were able to step up and make a difference.

As we stand tall and firm for all that is good and clean and whole-some, other mothers within our communities will take notice and want that goodness in the lives of their own families. They too will be sick and tired of the degrading messages the world offers and want to find a refuge, a place of safety for their families. They will want the light that emanates from you and your family to be a part of them and their family.

President Kimball prophesied that in the last days before the coming of Christ, it will be the righteous women of the church who will be the driving force behind the growth of the Church. You may be asking yourself, *How?* President Kimball answers, "In the last days . . . many of the good women of the world . . . will be drawn to the church in large numbers." But he says:

> This will happen to the degree that the women of the Church reflect righteousness and articulateness in their lives and to the degree that the women of the Church are seen as *distinct* and *different*—in happy ways—from the women of the world. Among the real heroines in the world who will come into the Church are women who are more concerned with being righteous than with being selfish. These real heroines have true humility, which places a higher value on integrity than on visibility. . . . It will be . . . female exemplars of the Church who will be a significant force in both the numerical and the spiritual growth of the church in the last days.[4]

Do you see how powerful we are as women? We have power to do great good in this world—which will not only benefit us, but more importantly, it will benefit our children, their friends, our neighbors, and all those who are within our sphere of influence for generations. But this will only happen *to the degree* that we will stand up and speak out for everything that is good and noble in this world. "It is not enough just to be good. We must be good for something. We must contribute good to the world. The world must be a better place for our presence. And the good that is in us must be spread to others."[5]

Sheri Dew once told of a time when a young woman walked up to her and said, "Sister Dew, when you wake up I'll bet the adversary says to himself, 'Oh heck, she's awake again.'"[6] Sister Dew went on to explain that hearing that comment gave her a new daily goal and objective: to beat the snot out of Satan every day. I believe *all* moms should have this same objective each and every morning we rise from our beds! We should wake up asking ourselves, "How am I going to fight against Satan today? How am I going to disrupt his evil plans this time?"

This great conflict being waged over the souls of men has been going on since before the dawn of time and we here today are experiencing its final stages. On the one side of the conflict is Satan—and he is fighting to enslave the souls of mankind. On the other side is Christ—and He is determined to save and liberate every last soul that that will allow Him to be their Savior.

We are all enlisted in this great conflict for the souls of men. Just by the sheer fact that we have been born on this earth puts us in the game of our lives. Only it's not a game. And if we're defeated, we can't stop the game and cry out for rematch. No. This is our time to prove ourselves.

The prophet Nephi warned that many Saints in this last dispensation would be lulled into carnal security. That many in our day would say, "All is well in Zion; yea, Zion prospereth, all is well" (2 Nephi 28:21). We cannot be mothers that fall for this false sense of security. We cannot be mothers who say "all is well with our families" and go on our merry way while Satan grasps his awful chains and slowly wraps them tightly around our children, binding their hearts to the things of this world. Binding their hearts to the things that cannot last and cannot give true and pure happiness.

As mothers in this generation, we need to step up our game! We cannot be oblivious bystanders while our innocent children are being dismantled by the world piece by piece. No! We need to stand tall, link arms with all like-minded moms, and shout out with all our might: "You will not take our children any longer!" And then proceed to go mama bear all over those institutions and practices that seek the spiritual death of our children.

Come on, moms . . . I know we can do it! Let's fight for our families! Let's show Satan once and for all that we are stronger than he is. That he is not welcome in our homes nor in our lives any longer, because we have dedicated them both to God. Be strong, be faithful, and always remember: "If God be for us, who can be against us?" (Romans 8:31).

REFERENCES

1. Edmund Burke: https://www.brainyquote.com/quotes/quotes/e/edmund burk377528.html.
2. Greg Trimble, "A Letter from a Dad to Carls Jr. and the Women in Their Commercials," last modified August 2014, https://www.gregtrimble.com/a-letter-from-a-dad-to-carls-jrs-and-the-women-in-their-commercials/.
3. Whitney Filloon, "Carl's Jr. Abandons Its 'Slutburger' Ads," Eater.com, last modified March 29, 2017, https://www.eater.com/2017/3/29/15105878/carls-jr-no-more-slutburger-ads.
4. Spencer W. Kimball, "The Role of Righteous Women," *Ensign*, November 1979.
5. Gordon B. Hinckley, *Standing for Something:10 Neglected Virtues That Will Heal Our Hearts and Homes* (New York: Times Books, 2000), 58.
6. Sheri Dew, *No One Can Take Your Place* (Salt Lake City, UT: Deseret Book, 2004), 11.

AFTERWORD

"The sweetest sounds to mortals given
Are heard in Mother, Home, and Heaven."
—WILLIAM GOLDSMITH BROWN[1]

Dear Moms,

So . . . never in a million years did I think I would ever write a book. Outside of adolescent school work, church lessons, and talks, I've never written anything in my life! The night Greg threw out the idea to me that I write a companion book to his, I *totally* blew it off and laughed at even the thought of me—ME—writing a book. *Yeah right!* But as I laid in bed later that evening, I couldn't sleep—I mean . . . at all! Thoughts and impressions wouldn't stop flowing through my mind and I knew I had to write them down before I forgot them.

I would write down a few thoughts on my phone's note tablet, then I would try to sleep. More thoughts would rush into my head, and I knew I should write them down too. This same process went on over and over and over again until I finally looked at the clock and it read 5:00 a.m.! In panic, I begged Heavenly Father to help me be able to fall asleep. I knew I was going to be totally wiped out for my ensuing interfaith *Faith in Motion* meeting the next morning.

I was afraid I would be snoring in the conference room surrounded by my pastoral friends and community social worker associates. I dreaded the thought of being the first "faith partner" in the history of Faith in Motion to actually fall asleep in my chair while the chairman of the Department of Social Services was expounding upon how to collect donated beds for children in need! And there I am, a faith partner, hanging off my chair as though it were a bed.

No thank you! That probably wouldn't paint too good a picture for the LDS church in showing how much we care about our community here in Riverside, California! Surprisingly though, when I woke up (about an hour after I was finally able to fall asleep), I felt energetic, lively, and ready to take on the day—undeniably a tender mercy from the Lord!

When Greg got home later that evening, I mentioned to him my experience of the night before. I told him that maybe I am supposed to write this book—*maybe*! I told him that I would work on the book if I kept feeling inspired to, and when or if I ever finished it, I would send it in to his publishers to see if they wanted it. I made him promise me that he wouldn't mention it to his publishers until I finished it.

It's never a good thing when your husband walks into the room, looks you in the eye and says, "Hun, you're going to kill me!" Yes, a week after I made him promise that he wouldn't talk to his publishers, guess what? He talked to them about the idea and they loved it! Not because they thought I was some talented writer—yeah, right . . . far from it. They knew nothing about me except that I was married to Greg. But they loved the idea of a companion book to Greg's book and figured I would be a great candidate since I was married to the author.

They ended up calling me the next day and asking how far along I was in my manuscript. "Manuscript . . . *what*?" My manuscript consisted of a few notes written on my phone in the middle of a long night! Long story short, they asked me to sign a contract and gave me four months to write this book. Did I mention that I've never written anything before in my life? Yeah, no pressure at all!

Writing this book was literally the hardest thing I've ever had to do. Each and every page I've written has been filled with my insecurities and I've wondered how I was actually going to accomplish this seemingly insurmountable task. I have no clue if this book will end up helping anybody or if anyone will even read it. But I do know that if nothing else . . . it has blessed my life and that of my family. And that's worth the struggle and stress. I have felt guided continuously and have fervently begged—literally begged the Lord relentlessly for

His guidance and assistance. I have felt it along the way. I've felt my normally cluttered mind become clear, and words just flow through my mind like rays of sunlight shining through the clouded recesses of my mind. Strokes of intelligence, as Joseph Smith would call it. I can't tell you how many times I would suddenly wake up in the middle of the night with thoughts flowing to my mind. I would quickly grab my computer and start jotting down what words were flowing to me. This was a constant occurrence throughout this book. I guess that's when the Spirit could get through to me the most. When my conscious mind was shut down and He could just speak through me.

In this book, I tried to speak to all women in every stage of the motherhood spectrum. To you young women, who are in the preparation stages of motherhood. To you young mothers, who are just opening up the new chapter of motherhood in your lives. And to all you seasoned mothers out there, who could use a little recharge of your motherly battery. I tried my best to speak to each of you.

I had a number of other chapters in mind that I was hoping to include in this book. The doctrine that all women carry the divine role of mother, whether or not they have children of their own in this mortal state, as well as the importance of grandmothers in the lives of their grandchildren: these are just a couple of the many chapters I was hoping to include in this book. Due to deadline constraints, I was not able to address these topics. Perhaps another time I will have the opportunity to speak on these other important issues affecting motherhood.

But for now, I hope you enjoyed this book and that you were able to get at least a little something out of its pages. Thank you for trusting me with your precious time.

Greatest blessings to you and your dear family.

WITH HIGHEST REGARDS,
KRISTYN TRIMBLE

REFERENCE

1. William Goldsmith Brown in Richard L. Evans, *Richard Evans' Quote Book* (Salt Lake City, UT: Publishers Press, 1971), 13.

ABOUT THE AUTHOR

Kristyn Trimble is a Southern California native who is obsessed with improving families through study and service. She considers one of her greatest gifts to be "the ability to love" other people. She is a regular contributor to her husband's blog (www.gregtrimble.com) and has been interviewed by *Deseret News* for her contribution to that site. Kristyn is currently a homeschooling mom and a volunteer for the world-renowned Millennial Choirs & Orchestras. She is in charge of leading the Women of Faith council in her region and participates in a wide range of interfaith committees and activities.

Above all, Kristyn loves hanging out with her family. She would consider herself a simple person and a natural introvert who is striving daily to get out of her shell. She loves reading, hiking, camping, and going on road trips.